to Stan
because you have
because I do
from Marylou
Merry Christmas, 1976

Also by WILLARD GAYLIN

The Meaning of Despair:
Psychoanalytic Contributions
to the Understanding of Depression

In the Service of Their Country:
War Resisters in Prison

Partial Justice:
A Study of Bias in Sentencing

CARING

CARING

WILLARD GAYLIN, M.D.

ALFRED A. KNOPF
New York   1976

THIS IS A BORZOI BOOK
PUBLISHED BY ALFRED A. KNOPF, INC.

Portions of this book originally appeared in
Psychology Today and *The Hastings Center Report.*

Library of Congress Cataloging in Publication Data

Gaylin, Willard.   Caring.
Bibliography: p.
Includes index.
1. Love. 2. Developmental psychology.
3. Psychology, Religious. I. Title.
BF575.L8G38   1976   155.4'18   76–13693
ISBN 0–394–49785–6

Manufactured in the United States of America

FIRST EDITION

FOR BETTY, JODY AND ELLEN

in gratitude and love

ACKNOWLEDGMENTS

I am indebted:

To the Hastings Center (and Daniel Callahan in particular) for that rare atmosphere of give-and-take, where new ideas can be imposed on old friends, and in that process be tested, refined, or abandoned.

To those inspiring while not unsparing critics whose patient foraging in the thicket of preliminary drafts enriched the final product—Andrew Heyward, Robert Michels, Margaret Steinfels, Peter Steinfels, and of course, my editor, Robert Gottlieb. Good friends all.

Finally, and completely, and as always—to my wife.

CONTENTS

CHAPTER I: Decline and Fall   3

CHAPTER II: *Sui Generis*   14

CHAPTER III: Helpless and Dependent   28

CHAPTER IV: The Nature of Nurture:
              Food and More   46

CHAPTER V: Attachment   64

CHAPTER VI: Separation   79

CHAPTER VII: Identification   94

CHAPTER VIII: Conscience   115

CHAPTER IX: Feeling   137

CHAPTER X: Despair   154

CHAPTER XI: Hope   166

              Bibliography   181

              Notes   193

              Index
              follows page   199

CARING

CHAPTER I

Decline and Fall

We live in a time of self-doubt. We are unhappy with the world we occupy and unsure of our capacity to change it. We are losing faith not just in our institutions, but in ourselves. Frustrated and insecure, we fix responsibility on our very nature—for the environment in which we reside is, in great part, our own creation. Anxiety about the future is generating guilt about our past, and present action and guilt will erode that self-pride and self-respect on which all human survival ultimately depends.

The medieval man, faced with the plague whose visitation he could not control, whose devastating ravages seemed purposeless, whose causes were unclear, and which he could neither control nor understand, conquered his anger and fear by embracing his own guilt in hopes that it would appease the demanding God he had offended, or exorcise the evil within that was threatening him. And we find ourselves now doing the same thing. But it is time we stopped flogging ourselves. Sanctimonious acts of public penance, like the self-flagellation of the dark ages, may lead inadvertently to the inflicting of real self-harm. For this time we attack not the individual but the species, and the mortification is not of the flesh but of the spirit and nature of man.

The scholarly community has been an accomplice to our self-denigration. The groves of Academe often resemble an intellectual jungle stalked by tigers and foxes competing to devour our reputations. And we embrace this situation because we have fallen out of favor with ourselves. It is not only fashionable but in a peculiar way reassuring to embrace the concept that *Homo sapiens* is an aggressor and destroyer whose destructiveness, until now, had been confined only by the somewhat limited scope of his power and the restraining influences of the institutions of civilization—from wherever those are supposed to have arisen.

We are a failure in our own eyes—and that is always a dangerous situation, whether for the individual or the species. A sense of failure is always defined in relationship to our aspirations; our despair, the ashy residue of our hope. The nineteenth century was indeed the century of great expectations. No man has hoped for more, or expected more, of himself than the nineteenth-century man. Certainly there were voices of pessimism then, too, but the general sense of the time was one of dazzling achievement and prideful accomplishment, and an assumption that more of the same would follow. By the turn of the century, Western man appeared to himself as the master of the world. He had control of the forces of nature; he was about to solve all the problems of his existence by application of his intellect.

German philosophical idealism was an elegant expression of this mood. It encouraged us to visualize the world we occupied as a world of our own creation, and while those idealists may have humbly suggested another real world out there beyond cognition, that world became an unattended postscript. Our true sensitivities and judgments, then as now, were defined by our perceptions, not our abstractions. The German philosophers assumed that we would find God through ourselves, but instead we have discovered God in ourselves; if the world was our creation, then we were its creator—only an article away from *the* creator.

The nineteenth-century man saw himself as a godlike

figure with almost unlimited potential powers who must merely avoid the crime of hubris. Compare this with the twentieth-century man. No longer the arrogant and self-confident creator, potential rival of God, we now perceive ourselves as, if anything, the destroyers of the world. We view ourselves as trapped in a society which, while necessary for our survival, we are nonetheless unsystematically and uncontrollably dismantling.

It is not feasible here to expand on all the possible reasons for this decline in self-esteem. Instead I will only suggest briefly those few that seem most pertinent to our purposes. Certainly, the success of science has proved to be a mixed blessing. The Frankenstein myth is a central metaphor in describing how success has reduced, rather than enhanced, our self-image. In 1818, when Mary Shelley first published her story, the scientific domination of society was just beginning. The idea of one human being fabricating another was purely metaphorical. The feat was presumed to be impossible, a grotesque exaggeration which cast in the form of a gothic tale the author's philosophical concern about man's constant reaching for new knowledge and control over the forces of nature. It was, to use her words, a "ghost story"—a fantasy to frame a poetic truth. But by the twentieth century the inconceivable had become conceivable. We find ourselves, indeed, patching human beings together out of parts.

At the time of the creation of Dr. Frankenstein, science was all promise. The technological age existed primarily in the excitement of anticipation, and there was leisure to philosophize. Man was ascending, and the only terror was that in his rise he would offend God by assuming too much and reaching too high—by coming too close. The scientist was the new Prometheus. By the end of that century, technology had surpassed even its own expectations. There was nothing that technology would not eventually solve. Man was too arrogant to recognize even arrogance. Man did not have to fear God, he had replaced him. The whole of history seemed to be contrived to serve the purposes and glorify the name of *Homo sapiens.*

It seems grossly unfair that so short a time should have produced so precipitous a fall. But, then, the way down the mountain has traditionally been faster than the way up. The tragic irony is not that Mary Shelley's "fantasy" is still relevant; the tragedy is that it is no longer fantasy, and that in its realization we no longer identify with Dr. Frankenstein but with his monster.

It was not the biological revolution that initiated or created our most intense anxieties and distrusts. That honor would have to be reserved for the world of physics. The image of the frightened scientist, guilt-ridden over his own creations, achieved its greatest credibility with the explosion of the first atomic bomb. The revulsion of some of the idealistic men who were involved in the actual making of the bomb, or in the theoretical work that led to it, has had a demonstrable influence on the scientific community and the broader world of ideas from the 1950's until now. The anxiety has mounted with the giant strides of the new biology of recent years, with its promise of genetic engineering, *in vitro* fertilization, rented womb space from surrogate mothers, artificial body parts, and so on.

If the success of technology has created problems, so has our sense of its failure. Our technology offered too many promises that were realized in the specific only to be lost when weighed as part of the total. Where was the promise of the nineteenth century to remove pain, hunger, suffering? There has been a general disillusionment, invoked perhaps by a recognition of continuing social injustice in the face of the successes of science.

Ironically, the very technologies which offered answers to certain problems created other problems to compound them. The ecology disaster was the most recent shattering blow, forcing us into a new sense of humiliation. The unexpected side-effects of our new technologies are not simply incidental and casual accompaniments of our new necessities; they are serious—deadly serious. The vehicles and discarded wrappings of our conveniences are killing us. We are used to throwing things out, but now, just as our garbage is becoming progressively more poisonous, we find ourselves running out of "out." Out is where we live, or where our children may be condemned to live.

The abandonment of religious faith which accompanied the rise of science has been suggested by William Barrett as the fundamental problem facing twentieth-century man. This, too, may have been born in a confidence that approached arrogance. Like the little red hen, we felt that those who failed visibly to contribute to the efforts of our success should not / need not share in the credit or the fruits of our labor. The accomplishments were man's—not God's. This being the case, when the fall came, where could we look for the authorship of our defeat; on whom could we project the burden and responsibility of the failures; to whom could we turn for succor and salvation?

Self-doubts and confusion also arise on a personal scale, here, in great part due to some unanticipated effects of the upwardly mobile society. In the traditional Old World society, a person knew that he could not leave the role, station, or often even the locality that was defined for him by the accident of his birth. He generally accepted his social class as he accepted his height. It was a part of him not to be questioned nor necessarily to be abjured. If his father was a baker, he became a baker; indeed, in the same shop with his father. For a woman, the role was the same, whatever her father did.

Constrictive it certainly was, but on the other hand, it had its compensations. To be a success in life, to have achieved his goal in such a society, all a man had to do after all was to be a good baker. In an upwardly mobile society, unlimited opportunities seem to be present (albeit less than meet the eye). The carpenter's son becomes free to become a cabinet-maker or even a manufacturer—and the same now with the carpenter's daughter. To be a success means not "succeeding," but surpassing the parent. In the fixed society, it was not uncommon to compliment a man by telling him he was almost as good as his father. In the upwardly mobile society, the previous generation is never the symbol of success; more often, it is the paramount symbol of failure. The parent in our society will insist that his child work harder, lest "you end up like me."

The advance in technology has compounded the problem described above. In many areas it has meant that the methods of the father are no longer transferable to the son, since they have in fact become inferior. In too many fields the methodology of even a few years ago seems archaic today. We can take the profession of medicine as one example. None of us physicians would be particularly willing to follow those earlier models of practice. We may want to follow some of the ideals of the nineteenth-century physician and to regain some of the humanity that we seem to have lost along the way, but certainly not the techniques and tools our predecessors used in treating specific conditions. Technology has often made the past seem irrelevant, and sometimes even foolish. In this sense there is a reality factor rather than a psychological one which makes it difficult to identify with the father as a success.

The myth of upward mobility implied that each generation not only had the opportunity, but an obligation to surpass the previous one. The ever-increasing opportunity seemed to demand increasing achievement in a society which still had very limited room at the top and carried with it the possibility of an ever-enlarging sense of one's own inadequacy. If you moved up a notch, why not the notch above; and if success is always defined by the notch above, then the notch we occupy is always the position of failure. Further, in the land of opportunity, failure is always of one's own making. If one analyzes the self-recrimination and social despair prevalent in so much current literature, whether it is self-oriented or species-oriented, it bears remarkable similarity to the self-deprecation of the depressed patient. And as with that depression, it is born of impotent rage, a feeling of abandonment and unworthiness, a sense of failure.

If it is true that our technology has run out of its adaptive course and purposes, as many fear, then it bears comparison with certain analogies in nature. In the Darwinian model of self-improvement, certain elks, over the years, developed larger and grander horns. The larger-horned elks, intimidating their competitors and attracting more females, won the battle for survival by virtue of this self-glorifying and self-enhancing equipment. Eventually, with selective breeding over generations, the horns became still larger and more elaborate until they were so complex and grand that they trapped the elk in the trees of the forest that were his natural habitat, and the species began to die out. What had originated as adaptive had become destructive.

Man's technology at this stage may indeed be seen as the horns of the elk. We have indications that technological society may have estranged us from certain limits of normal functioning so that, unawares, we have passed the apex and slipped onto the downward slope of the curve of utility. That which formerly was our glory and power—serving to enhance us—has begun to reduce us. We feel progressively impotent in the face of the pleasureless social institutions which we ourselves created but which now seem to control us.

It is no wonder then that following the holocaust, the atom bomb, the Vietnam War, continuing famines and profound inequalities of living standards, persistent bigotry and battery—it is no wonder that we welcome the prophets of doom who describe all these horrors if not as the inevitable, at least as the likely, products of the very nature of man.

We embrace this concept, furthermore, because in a perverse sense, if one cannot be really good, there is always a peculiar pleasure in being really bad. We embrace it also in a counterphobic way, pleading to be told that it is not so. We embrace it with the self-indulgence of self-pity, and we embrace it, finally, because if it is indeed the nature of our species that has brought us to this state, then our individual responsibility is mitigated.

It is not surprising, therefore, that many current students of human nature from the fields of anthropology, sociology, and biology, and particularly from the new field of ethology, have tended to emphasize the hostile, territorial, aggressive aspects of human behavior. Nor is it surprising that such scholarship has been popular in the common marketplace of ideas. But we accept these ideas at risk, and it is time to reconsider this one-sided evaluation of human nature.

Even were the case for the aggressive and hostile character of human nature made initially convincing, it would still be a false vision because of grave failures of omission. Such a pessimistic view must be balanced by one which has received little attention: the extraordinary capacity of the human being for loving and caring. If there is one fact founded in his biology, essential to his survival and uniquely his own, it is that *Homo sapiens* is supremely a loving animal and a caring one. If we properly contemplate the evidence which supports these positive aspects of human nature, it may direct us back to the very same behavior from which we have been inferring aggression; examining it from a different angle may reveal a different aspect, a more benevolent construction, of the same events.

Johann Fichte has said that what system of philosophy you hold depends wholly upon what nature of man you are. But we also know that what system of philosophy you hold will determine what nature of person you are to become. Psychological definitions tend to become self-fulfilling prophecies. It is part of our human strength to be able to redefine our nature. If we are convinced that we are innately evil, we will design the institutions of our culture according to that definition. John Gardner, the novelist, has said: "We live by the myths imposed on us, like actors in an endless play"; but more likely we live by the myths we impose upon ourselves. There is, therefore, an urgency to reexamine the questions of the nature of man. The wide acceptance of the positions popularized by Konrad Lorenz *et al.* was established at least as much on our readiness to hear their sermon as on the nature of the evidence itself; we must look once again into ourselves, and brace ourselves for good news. I do not deny that there may be a genetic directive for aggression in mankind, but the genetic basis for love is far more obvious, and that is what I plan to explore here. Man's great concern about his own aggression being innate does not necessarily prove that his aggression *is* innate, but such a concern suggests that care and love lie behind it. A ruthlessly aggressive animal would not have built into his nature so much anxiety about the presence of that aggression.

Man represents an incredible gap in "the great chain of life," a discontinuity that is not measurable in the traditional incremental changes from the lowest species of animal to the highest. We are as unlike the ordinary creatures of the earth as God, if He exists, must be unlike us. We are a splendid and peculiar discontinuity—*sui generis*. And there is drama in our development. For part of our uniqueness rests in the miserable, extended, helpless state in which we are born and remain for so long—untoward in the extreme, and unparalleled in the animal kingdom. For these miserable beginnings we are permitted to ascend to:

> Dominion over the Fowls of the Air, and the Beasts of the Earth and the Fishes of the Sea . . .

And as T. H. White has the Creator continue:

> . . . You, Man, you will be a naked tool all your life, though a user of tools. You will look like an embryo until they bury you, but all the others will be embryos before your might. Eternally undeveloped, you will always remain poten-

tial in Our Image, able to see some of Our sorrows, and to feel some of Our joys. We are partly sorry for you, Man, but partly hopeful.

We will start that ascent to nobility from the lowest state of dependency, and each step will pave the way for the next so that we may in turn become the kind of mature adult who will permit the next generation to repeat that cycle. The human infant gropes for care and protection, for the nurture that is essential to its survival and must be supplied by caring agents. Through that nurture, the infant will learn to cling and attach to this giving parent and will live in a state that approximates symbiosis. Borrowing strength from the loving parent he will learn the courage to bear separation, for ironically it is only in such separation—with all of its anxieties—that one can explore the world and begin the process of self-confidence and pride that leads to an independent state.

It is again part of the deviousness of human development that in order to achieve independence, a new kind of dependence is necessary as an intermediary. This new fusion, called identification, is unlike the early symbiosis with the parent. It is not a matter of "attachment to" but more a "becoming like." This new relationship, no longer attachment but not yet love, is essential for our development into the kinds of people who can learn to love others beyond self-love. It is necessary for the creation of an adult generation of people who are capable of endowing their offspring with care, thus ensuring the survival of the species.

It is an essential step, this identification, in our learning to "love" with all of the other meanings of the word. But even when we learn the marvelous mature manifestations of love, we will cling to our need for caring and being cared for. We will be "touched" by signs of caring and "hurt" by signs of indifference. When we feel unworthy of care and love, we will despair and perish; when we sense our worthiness, there will be the hope in our lives that is necessary for hope in the future. This, then, is the natural progress of the pilgrim in his quest to fulfill his biological purpose. This is the progress I wish to examine in this book.

Such reexamination is not designed to romanticize the current state of our affairs, but may, I hope, point the way to conclusions which are more compassionate, and solutions which are more effective, because of, rather than in spite of, the optimism of the view that supports them. Man cares because it is his nature to care. Man survives because he cares and is cared for. We may hypothesize that it is of our nature to destroy our own kind, but this will always remain purely a hypothesis. We will never surely know whether our destructiveness is an essential quality of our nature that has been controlled with only moderate effectiveness by our culture and institutions; or whether that same culture and those same institutions have imposed this dangerous quality on man's blessed but dangerous mutability. But the goodness inherent in man is no theory. It cannot be a *product* of culture because no species constructed as peculiarly as man could have survived to a point of culture without possessing at its core a supremely loving nature. Rather, we must see our culture and institutions themselves as being derived from the caring aspect of our species' nature. Civilization is, at least in part, a form of crystallized love. And it is time now that we begin to examine the case for caring and for love.

CHAPTER II

Sui Generis

A recent discussion between scientists and theologians at an interdisciplinary conference on the "nature of man" could have been a replay of the Scopes trial. Half of the group insisted on seeing *Homo sapiens* as one (albeit the highest) in a continuous line in the animal kingdom, while the other half of the group insisted on the uniqueness and special quality that separates the human being from all other creatures. Only this time it was the theologians, in defense of the rights of animals and nature, who were defining man as merely another animal variant; it was the scientists who—while not quite speaking of "man in God's image"— used their equivalent terminology when they referred to man as a "glorious discontinuity."

The scientific revolution may have been in part responsible for the cultural abandonment of the central role of God in the order of things, or perhaps it has only redefined that central figure. The same explosive expansion of knowledge and power which seemed to reduce the traditional God, elevated man to such a position that he assumed the perquisites of deity without any of the supernatural qualities. Now at this late date we have discovered the deficiencies of this deity, and we feel betrayed by the illusion we created. Since "we" are the illusion, it is a humbling and humiliating experience.

There is always a tendency to derogate the second best. If it is not all, it is nothing. And indeed there is some real danger in second best; the big loser in the poker game is the "almost best" hand, not the ordinary ones. But to be a rival to God implies a grandeur inconceivable in any other of his creatures, and places the human being in a limbo between creature and creator. Not necessarily farther from one than from the other, he is half animal and half ideal.

The special qualities that elevate *Homo sapiens* are in great part functions of that remarkable and little understood organ, the human brain. It is the brain which permits that true conceptual thought most commonly mentioned as the crux of humanness. Julian Huxley observed that:

> Conceptual thought could have arisen only in a multicellular animal, an animal with bilateral symmetry, head and blood system, a vertebrate as against a mollusc or an arthropod, a land vertebrate among vertebrates, a mammal among land vertebrates. Finally it could have arisen only in a mammalian line which was gregarious, which produced one young at birth instead of several, and which had recently become terrestrial after a long period of arboreal life.
>
> There is only one group of animals which fulfills these conditions. . . . Thus, not merely has conceptual thought been evolved only in man; it could not have been evolved except in man.

This ability for conceptual thought has been defined in numerous ways. It is often described in terms of our capacity to symbolize, to allow us to see the most abstract of signs as a representation of the true thing. And this capacity is observed in that most sparkling of examples, language. True speech, despite recent research on dolphins and chimpanzees, probably is exclusively human. True speech is not the utterance of sounds to communicate emotions to your fellows. Obviously, any dog lover knows when his dog is hungry, wishes to play or to go out. What the dog does not make explicit through his utterances (although the owner through his intelligence, his experience, and his capacity for abstractions may well know) is what he is in the mood for eating at the moment; what particular game he would prefer to play; where he wishes to go, and whether it is specifically for the purpose of urination, defecation, or simply to enjoy the evening air.

The capability for true speech has often been specified as the primary index of a capacity for conceptual thought. But it is only the expressive, communicative half of that capacity. Equally as important is its subjective, perceptual, and experiential aspect. For example, the capacity for symbol formation permits us to learn from the past and anticipate a future. We need not wait for the actual event but can utilize symbols, signs, or antecedents of the event as though they were the actual occurrences.

This is a mixed blessing; often what we read as symbols of the event will be true ones, but at times they will be our own distortions. It is a cliché of modern psychiatry that we truly live in a world of our own creation. One of the soundest distinctions between neurosis and health is that the healthy individual is for the most part capable of learning from (or at least responding to) experience. The neurotic cannot. In the area of his neurosis he never genuinely experiences the actuality of his life, but imposes a distortion from his past. Because of his capacity for symbolic recall, his memory may possess a greater reality to him than the actuality in which he is involved.

The paranoid individual, for example, does live in a world of hostile individuals by whom he is always cheated. To begin with, he will always recognize those incidents in which he has been short-changed in life in a way that most of us will not. Secondly, whether he is cheated or not, he always assumes he has been, and he will interpret each ambiguous, nonmeasurable, or arbitrary action as a calculated decision not in his favor. In his view, he is always given the smaller piece of pie, and he might just as well be in reality. Thirdly, I suspect, although this is more difficult to prove, that he usually *is* given the smaller piece of pie. There is nothing like a paranoid, sullen and resentful, assuming that he will not get his due, for inviting exploitation. The paranoid assumes that the trusting person will be more taken advantage of; I suspect that he is taken advantage of less, and I know that he goes through life convinced that "People never take advantage of me." Ultimately, that may be more important than what he actually experiences.

Because of this capacity for symbolization, each individual's experience even under the same circumstances is substantially different from another's. We can never display a stimulus response pattern that has the predictability of a computer. The stimulus has special meanings garnered from our individual pasts that make even the simplest situation different for all of us. This is a limitation that some social scientists, in their eagerness for quantification and the academic or scientific respectability that it brings, have at their own peril failed to recognize.

This capacity for symbolization also permits an anticipation of the future to a degree unparalleled among animals. Such anticipation allows for strengths and stabilities beyond the fragility of cartilage, sinew, and bone. The advantages of anticipation and prediction are obvious, particularly in matters of survival. But this quality of human behavior permits us, not merely to protect ourselves from the future, but to modify the impending event itself. In this sense we are not just reacting to our environment but preshaping it. We are, to an extraordinary degree, determinants of our future, not merely anticipatory subjects of it.

Of course the future we imagine may be only of our imagination; may never come to exist; may be only the product, once again, of some symbolic distortion from our past. In that case we will be protecting ourselves against that which would never have come and, worse, may be facilitating that which we dread. We create the world we will be forced to live in and which will determine what we shall become. "By changing what he knows about the world man changes the world that he knows; and by changing the world in which he lives man changes himself. . . . Evolution need no longer be a destiny imposed from without; it may conceivably be controlled by man, in accordance with his wisdom and his values," writes the distinguished geneticist Theodosius Dobzhansky.

The capacity to anticipate the future is nowhere better realized than in the capacity to visualize death. Other animals, of course, experience fear, but it is unlikely that any of them have any sense of the relation of pain-to-morbidity-to-mortality. Certainly no animal has a sense of personal mortality and certainly not the need and capacity to deny this sense by weaving webs of hoped-for immortality.

The sense of our own limitation is, if not quite the burden of Cassandra, something akin to it. But unlike Cassandra, it is now we ourselves who will not believe the future that we accurately foresee—at least not that of our own death. "Of all the world's wonders, which is the most wonderful?" the Bhagavad Gita asks, and answers, "That each man, though he sees others dying all around him, never believes that he himself will die."

But if we do not believe that we will die, the price we pay is that existential angst that permeates and pervades, corrupts and modifies, so much of the harmless activity of our daily lives. This anticipation of death and the mechanisms we exploit to deny its reality may be seen as a forebear, and essential ingredient, of religion, creativity, and the arts. In the same way, survival-oriented anticipation may explain technology and science.

This leads us then to the second aspect of human nature that has been most extensively commented on, our capacity for technology. Man has been called the tool-using animal. All of the apparent aspects of human life which most remarkably distinguish our lives from those of lower animals are extensions of the ability to use our conceptual thought to evolve science and technology. With these tools, culture becomes a modifier beyond the qualities that gave birth to it. It may, as we have suggested, alter the very form of the human body and the future of the species. Certainly in these days when we are in the process of discussing direct intervention into the genetic mechanism—alteration and modification of genes—the technology could conceivably change the structure of the very organism that created it, either to allow for more splendid elaboration of life with technologies, or, in unanticipated side-effects, to reduce our status or destroy us.

Probably as significant as direct intervention in the genes is that other mechanism by which a developed culture and technology can influence heredity. Culture becomes a vehicle for passing on the acquired learning and experience of one generation to another, thereby constituting the base from which the next generation builds to a newer height of culture. This accretion of knowledge and expansion from generation to generation is certainly a uniquely human characteristic. In a peculiar way, acquired characteristics *can* be transmitted to our offspring; culture is our parallel mechanism of heredity. As Dobzhansky has put it, "Our genes determine our ability to learn a language or languages but they do not determine just what is said. The structure of neither the vocal cords nor the brain cells would explain the difference between the speeches of Billy Graham and of Julian Huxley."

Culture is not just another mechanism of adaptation; it is vastly superior to the biological mechanism which spawned it. It is more rapid and efficient. When genes are changed through mutation, the change is transmitted solely to the specific offspring—and only with generations of time enters into the species at large. Changed culture, on the other hand, as Dobzhansky points out, "may be transmitted to anybody regardless of biological parentage, or borrowed ready-made from other people. In producing the genetic basis of culture, biological evolution has transcended itself—it has produced the superorganic." In other words, the kind of brain capable of conceptual reasoning is not only the product of a certain development but is capable of dictating a future development.

We commonly think of our intelligence as our chief distinction, but we do a disservice to our self-understanding if we see human beings as special exclusively in this area. This intellectual development could not, as Huxley stated, have occurred anywhere but in man. And some of the other attributes of human beings which allowed for the development of intellectuality are in their own right marvelous and special, and have had profound influences on our nature and the course of our history.

Homo sapiens is, for example, unique in his sexuality. Sexual reproduction and indeed sexual intercourse are something we share with many lower forms of animal. But man is the only continuously (not, alas but thank God, continually) sexed animal. This means that in human beings there is no mating season and no distinct estrus. In many higher forms, while the male animal may be continuously sexed, the mating season is linked to the occurrence of estrus in the female, in whom sexual desire is linked to the potential for reproduction. Since copulation requires the involvement of two organisms (except in such intriguingly hermaphroditic forms as the earthworm), this becomes an effective way of limiting sexual involvement to specific mating periods.

The liberation of sexual pleasure from sexual reproduction has had a profound influence on all human activities. Even those who reject the absolute centrality placed by Freud and his followers on the sexual drive surely recognize the implications of sexuality as entirely different in human life than in the lower animals. The complexity of this discussion is well beyond the scope or purpose of this chapter but, again, some details are worth noting. In lower animals it is the female animal in which estrus and desire are bound to reproductive capacity. With the change in *Homo sapiens* we are in exactly the opposite case. Women have been liberated from their estrus, but ironically, while now free to be receptive to sexuality continuously, have been made vulnerable to a cultural deprivation of pleasure. It is not necessary for a woman to enjoy the sexual act, for her to have desire, or even interest, in order to be fecund. This makes her vulnerable to rape and, perhaps more important, allows the potential development of cultural institutions to strip women of their sexual drive and their sexual pleasure, as in the attempts of Victorian sexual morality, where for purposes of economic or social stabilization, or merely exploitation, women were intimidated out of their innate biological capacity for sexual pleasure.

Ironically, with the introduction of the massive cultural privileges afforded to the male animal, he too has had to pay a price. It is true that the nature of his sexual organs makes him safe from rape by a woman—a culture would last only one generation if it deprived its male population of the right to sexual pleasure, for fecundity in men is closely tied to desire and passion. A man cannot, without laboratory assistance, conceive a child without being in a sexual mood; an erection is necessary for penetration. But, here, in exactly the reverse situation from the lower animals, where the female finds her capacity for sexual pleasure controlled by her ability to procreate, the male animal finds his ability to procreate controlled by his sexual pleasure.

Another unique aspect of human sexuality is in the range of fertility: few animals are capable of such variation as the human species. Women can range within their life spans of fertility from being capable of having zero to fifteen, eighteen, or twenty offspring. In fact, the rate of infertility in human beings is the highest in the higher primates.

Another sexual distinction is in the length of "post-maturity" existence. This difference is two-dimensional. In *Homo sapiens*, a much larger percentage of the total population survives past its reproductive capacity. If the practical reproductive capacity of a woman is roughly between the ages of fifteen and forty-five, we have a fertile period of about thirty years. But the life expectancy of women in our culture is about seventy-five, leaving thirty years more of survival. In the female of the species, at least, the post-maturity era is now as great a percentage of the life span as the era in which she is capable of producing children. Similarly, there is a greater percentage of older people in the human population than in other animal populations. In most other animal groups, very quickly after the productive era the animal dies or is abandoned by the group. In the human population, not only is the older animal not abandoned by the group; he is prevalent, and is often the most powerful member of the group in terms of positions of control, accretion of capital, authority, and the like.

Of course, the human being also has a much longer life span than most other higher animals. The extended post-reproductive period, combined with our long life span, allows for another unique attribute of human life: the coexistence in time of two and even three adult generations. This co-existence served as a powerful force to initiate that para-biological mechanism of transmitting acquired knowledge just described, before the development of writing. It was this capacity to communicate orally across generations—because we coexisted in time—that allowed the culture to grow sophisticated enough for us to invent writing. I suppose that now we have written (and recorded and filmed) records, there is no longer a biological necessity for an older genera-tion. While the roots of the precipitous decline in respect for the elderly in the last seventy-five years probably lie in other areas, this erosion of a significant cultural role makes the sociological abandonment of the older generation possible without the measurable damage it once would have done. I suspect we pay other prices for this ingratitude, no less dear for being less obvious.

Human beings are also the widest ranging of all animals. We cover distances unheard of by any other species and had done so even prior to the advance technologies which have now reduced the breadth of our continent to a four-hour trip.

Probably directly related to our range is the fact that we are the most variable of all species, with the exception of those artificial species which are also a product of man's technology, domesticated animals. We come in different sizes and different colors and different shapes. With all this variation we continue to breed true and to be capable of breeding amongst ourselves—this being the ultimate definition of a species. We have not fragmented into various species, each then either following its own true line, developing divergent patterns, or falling into extinction.

It is this that Julian Huxley has referred to as reticulate, rather than divergent, evolution. We have permitted this wide-ranging animal that is *Homo sapiens* to reconnect with its divergent kind in other sections of the world where other conditions have encouraged, by natural selection, different traits. This reconnection then allows for a further diversification. The pattern is constantly repeated and by this diverging, differentiating, converging, and recombining network, human descent evolves. Because we roam, because we can ignore in our mating vast differences in morphology inconceivable in lower forms, we become an extraordinarily diverse and enriched species. We identify "others" so different in shape and color as the same species, as a part of the "us," and we maintain these identifications through contact, communication, and so on. But, as Huxley has pointed out:

> Superposed upon this purely biological or genetic variability is the even greater amount of variability due to difference of upbringing, profession, and personal tastes. The final result is a degree of variation that would be staggering if it were not so familiar. It would be fair to say that, in respect to mind and outlook individual human beings are separated by differences as profound as those which distinguish the major groups of the animal kingdom. The difference between the somewhat subnormal member of a savage tribe and a

Beethoven or a Newton is assuredly comparable in extent
with that between a sponge and a higher mammal. Leaving
aside its vertical differences, the lateral difference between
the mind of, say, a distinguished general or engineer of
extrovert type and of an introvert genius in mathematics or
religious mysticism is no less than that between an insect
and a vertebrate. This enormous range of individual variation
in human minds often leads to misunderstandings and even
mutual incomprehensibility; but it also provides the necessary
basis for fruitful division of labour in human society.

While Huxley's examples may strike the modern reader as
arrogant or elitist, the unique fact of wide variability within
species is well documented.

Another distinction of *Homo sapiens* from the lower
animals is in the prolonged period from the moment of birth
to the moment of self-sufficiency or independence. This is,
of course, a difficult period to define. If one takes sexual
maturity as the point of maturation, however, the human
being spends roughly 20 per cent of his life reaching that
particular position (which is longer than any other species).
Ironically, the evolution of man via his culture has, if anything, aggravated the condition. While an individual is
biologically capable of reproducing his own kind at puberty,
anywhere from thirteen to fifteen years of age, we know that
he is incapable of assuming either the social or the economic
role of the parent in our modern technological society. So,
if anything, we have extended the period of childhood and
redefined it at a higher level than the already extended
biological base.

And if we take a period from birth to a point where we
could readily expect the individual, if not the species, to survive (independent of the artifacts of cultural institutions),
Homo sapiens is even more extreme in his period of helplessness. It is unlikely that a human child, dropped into a jungle
setting, could find the means to its own survival with any
statistical degree of reasonableness before the ages of ten or

twelve or very close to the pubescent period. So in addition to the age of reproducibility of kind, the age of autonomous functioning is also extraordinarily delayed in human beings.

Finally, the most unique aspect of human development is the total helplessness of the human infant and the uncharacteristically long period of time in which it remains floundering in this helpless state. Adolf Portmann, the distinguished student of animal behavior, has said:

> The most striking among those marks of our civilized state is the peculiarity of our early development. Instead of continuing in the protection of the mother's body as long as would accord with our superior brain development, we are born as helpless creatures—in contrast to the state in which most mammals are born. Instead of beginning our life with well-developed limbs and the ability to move as freely as grown-ups of the species—like deer, calves, foals, like elephant cubs, young giraffes, whales, dolphins and seals—we have a special extrauterine first year very different from our further development, during which we gradually learn both to stand and to talk through social contact; we also learn purposeful action, the specific human fashion of controlling environment. None of these three facilities will be fully achieved if social contact is lacking or inferior. That is one of the reasons why biologists are eager to bring up both the correspondences and the differences between the behavior of men and of the animals most closely related to him.

Portmann points out that relatively uncomplicated and undifferentiated animals are capable of birth with a short gestation period. A guppy must face life at the moment of birth. Autonomous and independent, it must avoid its first predator—its mother. More remarkably, a sea urchin is prepared to face a hostile environment only hours after the egg has been *fertilized.*

As one would expect, the more complicated the animal, the longer the gestation period, so that by the time we reach that relatively higher mammal, the elephant, we have a gestation period of twenty-two months. But: "It is a peculiarity of man that despite his higher level of differentiation he has to meet his environment far earlier than the elephant does."

From the standpoint of the psychological development by which we identify human beings as such, beyond mere physiological and physical description, this dependency period is crucial—crucial, that is, in the development of a person who loves and is lovable, who has emotions and relationships, is capable of altruism and hope. For while all these attributes are biologically rooted, they will be psychologically encouraged or destroyed in the lessons of dependency learned in our peculiar period of extended helplessness.

How is it, then, that man is born in such an utterly helpless state with practically no instinctual capacities for survival or self-preservation? Once again, we come full circle and return to that remarkable instrument of evolution, the human brain. The rapid physical growth of the human brain *demands* birth at nine months of gestation, otherwise it could not pass through the peculiarities of the birth canal necessitated by the upright posture of the human mother. In other words, given the nature of a human pelvis, and the extraordinary size of the fetal brain at nine months, it is essential that the fetus pass through at that time, even though this may mean that in comparison with other animals it is born with a peculiar and particular vulnerability. The human brain weighs roughly 350 grams at birth. By the end of the first year of life, it will have grown to 825 grams out of a total potential brain growth of 1,400 or less. Indeed, by two years of age it will reach over 1,000 grams.

It is for this reason that many authors have referred to the first year of life as a final stage of fetalization. This is merely a way of seeing gestation as having an intra-uterine and an extra-uterine period, comparable to the marsupials. Unlike the marsupials, however, *Homo sapiens* has no protective pouch—that "open uterus" to protect the fetus during this extra-uterine gestation. Nor is there the automaticity of development that occurs within the relatively constant and predictable environment of that pouch. Yet, one suspects, there must be some constant biological mechanism to protect so vulnerable a young. If there is no pouch, then the loving responses of the maternal organism must be its substitute. Otherwise, no species so designed could survive.

This prolonged early helplessness demands much from the parent and imposes a new set of rules in the relationship of the individual to his developing society. No other animal exists for so long a time in so helpless a state. And no helpless animal in its infancy is endowed with so much awareness; as the human child develops, he soon becomes cognizant of his utter helplessness—as well as his dependence on those around him, and their good will, for his survival. If gestation is considered to extend through the year beyond birth, it is a peculiar kind of gestation, for it is the gestation of an *aware* fetus who, while helpless to act, is not helpless to perceive, and with that perception is learning lessons he will never forget. Among those lessons, the most crucial one is the link between helplessness, care, and survival.

CHAPTER III

Helpless
and Dependent

It has been said, by those outside the field, that to psychoanalysts the first year of life is everything. Like most comments these days about psychoanalysis, this is an exaggeration. To a psychoanalyst like myself, the first year of life is *almost* everything. This first year is dominated by the utter helplessness of the infant, and his growing awareness of his dependency.

In that masterpiece of his later years, *Inhibitions, Symptoms and Anxiety* (1926), Freud discusses the crucial factors in human development.

> The biological factor is the long period of time during which the young of the human species is in a condition of helplessness and dependence. Its intra-uterine experience seems to be short compared to that of most animals, and it is sent into the world in a less finished state. As a result the influence of the objective world upon it is intensified and it is obliged to make an early differentiation between the ego and the id. Moreover the dangers of the outer world have a greater importance for it, so that the value of the object which can alone protect it against them and take the place of its former intra-uterine life is enormously enhanced. This biological factor, then, establishes the earliest situation of danger and creates the need to be loved which will accompany the child through the rest of its life.

"Dependency" is an ambiguous word with multiple meanings. Such words often get us into trouble, unless we know specifically to which definition we are attending. "Dependency" refers to an actual state of being, whether physical or psychological; it refers to an attitude and a self-evaluation, a method of adaptation; to a description of an interrelationship between people; to a mode of living, whether economic, sociological, or psychological; and more.

All these various meanings are interrelated and derive from a primal model. For the purpose of our discussion here it is to this primal model that we must attend: the state of utter helplessness of human infants, and their total incapacity to survive without the ministrations of the adult members of the community. Somewhere, sometime, it will be necessary for all the ramifications of the "dependency constellation" to be explored in detail from a psychoanalytic point of view. This has not been done yet, and cannot be done here. In what follows, "dependency" is treated merely as a vehicle for exploring, substantiating, and elucidating the caring nature of the human being.

One would think that dependency should have played a central role in any psychoanalytic theory of human development, but it has not. How such a factor, so closely linked to the biological nature of the species—to the very survival of that species—could be so ignored, raises real questions. The answer lies in a further paradox: even survival is a peripheral and neglected concept in traditional, early psychoanalytic literature. The explanation for this lies in the peculiar history of the psychoanalytic movement in general and of Freud's thinking in particular.

Psychoanalysis, until the recent advent of ego analysis, and perhaps even since, has been dominated by the genius and personality of Freud, and the force of his personality has transcended even the awesome impact of his theories. It is not surprising, therefore, that so many scholarly articles in early psychoanalytic literature read like theological disquisitions, the adumbrations of disciples on the doctrines of the Master. It is as though all psychoanalysis, until the most recent times, has followed the Talmudic tradition of allowing only elaborations on a central text. If Freud chose to ignore the linked factors of survival and dependency, then so too must those followers who saw themselves as commentators on The Word, rather than as creators or synthesizers of a new tradition.

It is not that Freud failed to recognize the central nature of the dependent state, as the quotation previously cited—and others—prove. In his writings in applied psychoanalysis where the insights of psychoanalysis are applied to social problems—the arts, culture, and history—Freud repeatedly alluded to the impact of the early state of helplessness. In *Civilization and Its Discontents* (1930), he clearly traced man's need for religion back to that original feeling of infantile helplessness.

It is in the central body of his psychoanalytic thought, whose primary concern, after all, was in developing the theory of neurosis, that the omissions are most glaring. Here the sexual instinct and its vicissitudes dominate the discussion of the nature of man to an overwhelming degree. Here is the libido theory on which all modern psychoanalysis was based: an instinctual theory, which essentially attempts to explain all development in terms of the internal conflict within the person, rather than in terms of his relationships. Of course Freud acknowledged that both sets of conditions existed, but the focus of his theoretical work was on the internalized struggle and the constitutional nature of human behavior. This choice of emphasis was to have an enormously enriching effect on Freudian theory. It permitted him—indeed, forced him—to study human development. It allowed psychoanalysis to become more than a limited tool for the treatment of restricted emotional disorders, permitting its development into a potent psychological explanation of normal human behavior.

On the other hand, this frame of reference did tend to take man out of his milieu, to force a concern with energy concepts which proved to be futile; and it allowed for the neglect of crucial aspects of human behavior, such as identification and dependency—aspects which were only to be recovered when Freud began another reevaluation of his work in the 1920's. Starting in 1905 with the publication of *Three Essays on the Theory of Sexuality*, the global model under which more technical theories developed was that of an instinctually (sexually) driven animal, in which conflicts with the environment precipitated defensive maneuvers; but it was these internal conflicts which caused neurosis. Neurotic conflicts arose from the internal struggles of "man against himself."

As I have said above, the conflicts with the environment were reserved as the focus for Freud's work in applied, rather than theoretical, psychoanalysis, in other words, his studies outside the medical model, where interest was directed to culture, religion, and other institutions of social living. Here, too, the instinct theory dominates. The instinct seeks for the gratification of release; in his drive for instinctual pleasure, the individual comes to grips with an often inhibiting and frustrating environment; the problem for the individual is to bring his drives under the control of a reality principle which necessitates either the frustration, inhibition, sublimation, or modification of those drives to meet the standards of the civilized world. This thesis was to reach its culmination in a book which was to have a profound effect on those sociologists and political scientists who examined the Freudian literature—the book was, of course, *Civilization and Its Discontents*. In this model, the essential image is that of an individual striving for gratification of (at this point) both aggressive and sexual drives, who is kept under control by the forces of civilization. This view of *Homo sapiens* depicts him as essentially individualistic and selfish, with civilization as the restraining force which has kept him in check.

The concept of individualism, which was born and thrived in the nineteenth century, particularly in America, was to achieve even further idealization in the twentieth century. But man is not, technically speaking, an individual. Man is an obligate social animal; a social structure is a part of his biology and a necessary part of his functioning. We are a social animal not by election but by nature. Precisely because of our prolonged dependency, we could not survive as a species or develop as a type were there not a social structure to support us. While man is not quite a colonial animal like coral, he is certainly also not a true individual like an amoeba. He rests somewhere in between, and no theory of the nature of man is complete that does not recognize the obligate social structure in which he must develop. It is to an earlier work of Freud's that we must return to find his acknowledgment of this.

Totem and Taboo (1912), in contrast with *Civilization and Its Discontents*, has had relatively little impact on modern thought. Its neglect is chiefly due to its being at least partly based on the Lamarckian concept of human hereditary mechanisms which Freud, in his ignorance, shared with many of his contemporaries.

Totem and Taboo was the first attempt by Freud to analyze the social structure and its relationship to human nature. And here the message is quite different from—indeed, almost antithetical to—that of *Civilization and Its Discontents*. For our purposes, the most important part of *Totem and Taboo* is the final, fourth section. Freud was interested at this time in examining the incest barrier in particular, but also the origins of certain religious rituals and taboos. This, then, is his first detailed study of organized morality. It draws heavily on Darwin's "primal horde" theory of the origin of society, but also on Atkinson's *Theory of Social Origin* derived from a study of ape populations.

Freud postulated the "scientific myth" that man once

existed in a primal horde, and that the understanding of the conditions of that existence might help to explain the evolution of certain moral principles. This primal horde with father, mother, and children became disrupted when the younger male members (brothers) clamored for sexual access to the females (mothers and sisters) in the clan. This eventually led, Freud postulates, to a revolt by the brothers; patricide; the eating of the father; and the reinstitution of male-dominant clans, but now with a sense of instability and fear that could destroy the base for social life. The disruption of the social system is thought, then, to be eventually recognized by some succeeding generation who, with a sense of guilt and horror, also recognized that the same thing might happen to them. The totemic taboos which prohibit killing of the totemic animal (symbol of the father) and the abolition of incest would be seen, then, partly as a subsequent obedience mechanism for handling guilt and partly as a recognition that order was necessary for the survival of all. "The incest barrier probably belongs to the historical acquisitions of humanity and like other moral taboos it must be fixed in many individuals through organic heredity." Freud, under the influence of Jung at this time, postulates that we have inherited the memories of that early primal horde situation, and through this inheritance we have established certain moral taboos and restrictions on behavior which will allow for civilized living.

We know that we cannot *inherit* memory traces from an ancestral past. But the actual mechanism is unimportant. Even the theory (the primal horde) from which it derives is unimportant. If one strips *Totem and Taboo* of these two specifics, the message becomes clear: certain revulsions, certain moral behavior patterns, are so essential for the survival of the species that they cannot be an accident of culture but must be built into the genetic nature of the species. To think otherwise, to shift certain moral behavior into the cultural area, is to make the survival of the species the luckiest of all accidents—and Freud no longer believed in "accidents."

What Freud has said about the incest taboo may or may not be true, but certainly something similar to it must be true about the protective, loving, caring attitudes of the adult human being toward the child. The first function of the guppy previously alluded to was to escape from its mother, who viewed it as perhaps an ideal postpartum feast. Were the attitude of the human mother, hungry and fatigued after birth, to be the same, one suspects that the peculiar mutation which is *Homo sapiens* would not have survived.

Other animal forms also respond to infantile creatures of their kind. One has only to observe a male dog aggressively approach a strange dog (often bigger than itself), then sheepishly retreat when it realizes that it is only a puppy, to know that there is a protective attitude toward the young built into many of the advanced species. But with the human organism the indulgence required is enormous, considering how long that human infant is helpless—and how incredibly helpless it is. It is enough to test the patience of a Job (who, not by accident, was a human being).

Nor can the protective attitude toward the young be designated merely a "maternal instinct," for surely the hungry father being physically stronger than the female of the species would also have seen the small object as a solution to his carnivorous appetites. Given the prolonged dependency period of human beings, it is unlikely that the protective response of the adult for the young would not be part of the genetic inheritance. To repeat, no species so designed could have survived the hundreds of thousands of years from its inception to a point of organized civilization where such codes of conduct might have been imposed and transmitted via cultural heritage, unless there had been from the beginning an innate genetic response of caring and loving for the helpless newborn. In *Totem and Taboo* Freud sets the structure for all culture and religion, manners and ritual, on the genetic and biological nature of the species.

Sandor Rado, a distinguished follower of Freud and a great early theoretician of the libido theory, eventually broke with that theory specifically on the issues of its neglect of survival and dependency. Yet despite the fact that he built a brilliant theory of psychopathology with a dependency adaptation at its core, he seemed to misunderstand the essential nature of dependency. To Rado, dependency was a neurotic means of problem resolution, and was his substitute for the concept of regression in classical Freudian literature. Both saw the return to patterns of childhood as inevitably sick or neurotic. Rado rooted his psychology in the emerging physiological literature of stress. He saw all reactions to danger as fight-or-flight reactions, according to the system of Walter Cannon. He then conceptualized an organism in whom survival was mediated either through fear or rage and the behavior they dictated: fight or flight.

But the human infant is capable neither of fleeing nor of fighting. The infant does not see his survival in avoiding the source of danger, which he does not even recognize, and surely not in overcoming the danger, which inevitably is beyond his limited coping capacities. Neither of these is a realistic option. The first method of survival is neither fight nor flight, but rather something that might be called clutch or cling.

It is impossible, of course, directly to establish the thinking of an infant; yet it is a worthwhile speculation, which many have attempted. Once one strips the technical language in which the ideas are wrapped from the essential substantive thought, there is a remarkable similarity in all the varying theories of developmental psychology that presume a consciousness and a cognition.

The earliest stage of childhood development may be referred to by some as a stage of primary narcissism, by others as magical omnipotence or what-have-you. But basic to most views of this period is an image of an infant who is aware of self and probably unaware of environment. Self-awareness may be seen as stemming from a number of different mechanisms. Some ascribe the first awareness to the mouth and the tactile stimulations of the lips arising in the feeding situation; others see the first self-awareness as rooted in the proprioceptive system of stretching and moving, which may manifest itself well before birth, thereby placing it before the establishment of orality. We do often sense "ourselves" through the positions of parts of our body in relationship to other parts. It is difficult for most people not trained in biology to understand the proprioceptive modality. We know what hearing, seeing, smelling, and touching mean, but the proprioceptive sense is more subtle. It is the sensation which permits us to know where our hand is in relation to our nose in that peculiar test neurologists ask us to perform. In telling us where one part is in relation to another part, it may define our limits. To define that which is a "non-part" is to separate self from environment.

At any rate, the earliest stage is dominated by the child's sensations, not yet necessarily even emotions. He senses needs and pains, hunger, discomfort, pinpricks, wetness, and so on. What is meant when we say the child is feeling hunger? Certainly the "concept" of hunger in the first days of life is unknown to him. What he is aware of is pain due to the gastrointestinal activity or even, possibly, to some psychic extension of that. He screams (rage?), and seemingly his scream produces—in time—a warm suffusion of liquid into the gastrointestinal tract, relieving the distress. The child is not aware of a complicated sequence of events that transpires between the scream and the alleviation of his distress. He cannot possibly know that the cry may awaken a somnolent father, who may then awaken a somnolent mother, who may then go through the detailed business of warming a bottle or preparing for nursing, and so on. The child's cry cannot be interpreted by him as a call for attention or a

plea for help. At this stage of his development, if any conceptualization is possible, it must be presumed that the conception is one in which the cry *itself* produces the satisfaction
desired. I myself recall an extremely early memory in which
I presumed that the way to convert night into day was to
close my eyes and then to immediately reopen them. It
seemed to me that the closing of the eyes followed by the
act of opening them caused the darkness to turn into light.
The concept of sleep, or even the awareness of elapsing time,
was not part of my conceptualization. This sense of self
alone, and in control of the satisfaction of one's needs, is
called magical omnipotence.

When the child begins to sense environmental factors, it
is likely that he will at first egocentrically identify them as
extensions of himself. Only gradually will the child become
aware of the environment around him as an alien entity—
and how his concept will then change! With the conceptualization of the environment, he becomes aware that not only
is he not magically omnipotent, he is not even potent. He is
totally powerless, incapable of ensuring any of his creature
comforts, let alone the essential needs of his survival. With a
fall that must rival the fall of the angels (perhaps inspiring
that myth?), he is reduced from the highest of creatures to
the lowest. It is the awareness of the child's relationship
to an environment distinct from himself that first brings to
consciousness a crushing awareness of helplessness and vulnerability. But this awareness is mitigated in turn by the
recognition of other figures in that environment who are
strong. The first differentiated figure is unquestionably the
mother; and while the child's sense of himself is limited, his
sense of her full powers is magnified. In relationship to the
limited needs of the infant, the capacities of the mother are
more than adequate for almost total satisfaction. It is presumed that the child then enters a stage of delegated omnipotence, overvaluing the parental figures and seeing them
now in the role in which he had formerly cast himself. There

are, indeed, awesome, powerful figures who occupy the universe. They may not be the child himself, but by some glorious happenstance they are capable of supplying him with all that he needs. It is they who have power over the environment, and fortunately they use this power for his purposes.

With time he will begin to learn that these parental figures not only have the power to give pleasure, to support needs, to satisfy desires, but also the power to withhold. Ironically, it is in the recognition of the discriminatory capacity, rather than the automaticity of the giving of parents, that the child will begin to sense his own power. He will begin to see that he too has, if not direct, at least derivative power via his influence with the adult figure. It is not just that the parents have the capacity to supply his needs; he now has the more sophisticated knowledge that they are *willing* to supply his needs. The child then learns that this willingness is related to the nature of their relationship with him and their feelings for him. The powerful parental figures are loving, and so long as they remain loving, that which he needs will be supplied by them. Awareness thus begins to build the mechanism which links dependency through love to survival. To be helpless is not necessarily to be in jeopardy. To be helpless *and unloved* is the matrix of disaster. The "power" of helplessness fuses with the "power" of lovability to become an essential part of the complicated dependency lessons that the infant will almost inevitably carry into his adult life.

If anxiety is first felt in the early days of life, it is surely not the castration anxiety which dominates much of later life—even in the symbolic sense in which it has come to be used in the psychoanalytic literature, i.e., the fear of reduction of potency and power by removal of the instruments of power. There are no instruments of power for male or female in the first years of life. The locus of power is in the other, and it is only with time that one becomes aware of one's own capacity for power. The first sense of our own power is experienced vicariously in the capacity to endear or ingratiate the all-powerful mother, thereby ensuring her loving presence. The first fear experienced by the individual in relation to his environment, therefore, must be separation anxiety. And indeed the image of terror to be seen on the face of a two-year-old child momentarily separated from his parent in a crowd is perhaps beyond that of any other routine circumstance people are likely to encounter.

This loving and caring capacity is obviously a complex one. That it may be limited in some individuals, that there are parents who beat, destroy, or simply do not tend to their children, is, of course, obvious. What is crucial is the degree to which this capacity is limited. If the deprivation is sufficiently severe, either the survival of the small human being, or the nature of his humanity, will be imperiled. But these occasional abnormalities cannot refute the inclination to caring clearly resident in the biological nature of the species.

The evidence for parental caring can be derived deductively from the fact that sacrifice of a child is often the highest price that can be asked of an individual—an asking usually reserved for the Creator. The greatest sacrifice is traditionally not one's own life, which is entered into willingly in many cultures, but the sacrifice of one's child. The tenth and most awful plague on the house of Egypt was the death of the first-born; when God wished to test Abraham, it was the sacrifice of Isaac that was demanded; the horrible price that Artemis demanded of Agamemnon was the death of Iphigenia; and, finally, the only offering sufficient to demonstrate the extent of God's love of man was the sacrifice of His Son.

We are caring people, despite the fact that it is fashionable now to deny it. How much of our capacity to care may have been damaged by our culture remains to be seen, but that some is left is observable in the everyday behavior of human beings as well as in biology and literature. We respond not only to the child, but the childlike; we respond to the helpless, whether animal or human. All forms which have an infantile representation are particularly capable of touching us. Witness the current campaign to preserve the harp seal, which inevitably features pictures of this plump, sad-eyed, soft, and cuddly creature. While bearing a certain sympathy for endangered species, I nonetheless ask you to consider that if the species endangered had the same name but a different form, would the campaign have been as effective? Suppose the young harp seal was a 30-pound animal which looked like a giant cockroach or beetle. Would we have responded to the pathetic plight of this "baby" if visualized, full-blown in *The New York Times*, with his beady eyes, hard shell, crawling antennae, and over-enlarged incisors? I suspect not. We are subject to an aesthetic bias which is very much related to the natural tendency to care for the young and to visualize *the* young in terms of *our* young. It is difficult to perform controlled experiments, but subjective evidence is at hand that the pug-nosed, blue-eyed, freckle-faced prototypic choirboy transgressor of the law inevitably will be seen in a different perspective from the pimply-faced, obese, and unattractive child of the same age. We associate innocence with a certain visual image (baby-faced?) that may go back to biological derivations. Granted there are other derivatives of aesthetic bias, but it seems clear that the large-eyed, small-featured, smooth-skinned quality associated with the innocence of babyhood is one strong component of our aesthetic bias. Certain features, prepubescent and soft, relate in our minds to innocence, and ultimately to helplessness; and it is the helplessness of the child which in all probability initiates a protective response in the normal adult. Again, it is important to recall that the human being is the least instinctually fixed animal on earth. We do not follow genetic imperatives, or very few; we hardly ever follow even genetic directives. It is testament to man's power, authority, and uniqueness that even nature only dares *suggest* to him future courses of action. So it is quite possible in the course of our development that many of us will obliterate even our response to helplessness and become desensitized to this as we are capable of desensitizing ourselves to other aspects of our personal potential. But there is ample evidence of a readiness, on an intuitive and almost reflexive pattern, to respond to the helpless of our species.

Similarly, I am absolutely convinced that there is a contagious quality to tears. If a grown man would uncontrollably begin to shed tears in front of a group of strangers, a choked reaction would be elicited in a number of them independently of the knowledge of what caused the tears. The capacity to respond to the visual image of the helplessness of others may well explain, among other factors equally important, the response to the death of the Kennedy brothers and Martin Luther King, Jr. The fact that we were capable of visualizing via the medium of television the distress of those around them added a greater reality and fuller identification with their tragedy. It is inconceivable to me that anyone, independent of political judgment or position, could have witnessed Senator Edward Kennedy's eulogy for his brother and, at the moment at which he seemed to lose control, when his voice began to break, not find a welling up of his own grief.

Symbols of separation have often been used as a visualization of the most dreaded state of man, whether it be in banishment from country or isolation from kind—Ulysses the wanderer or Leopold Bloom ("the only Jew in Ireland"), the Flying Dutchman or Ishmael; the person detached or separated from his loved ones, his protectors, his home, or his kind, is a tragic figure. Such separation is visualized as a fate comparable to death. Indeed, it may be that the principal way the human being is ultimately capable of visualizing death is via separation. For death is so terrible an absence that we tend to deny its existence. Since we are incapable of perceptualizing something without ourselves as the perceptualizing agent, we often see death not as the absence of us, but the absence of everything except us. It is the horrifying dream of being buried alive. Certainly the *child* is more threatened by withdrawal of love than by the foolish parent who might threaten to kill him. While death psychologically probably does not exist even for the adult, it most certainly does not exist for the young child. The withdrawal of love is close enough, and as such is a greater coercive force.

Beyond direct observation of the child, indeed preceding it, certain assumptions about childhood perceptions were made by psychoanalysts who observed both the unconscious fantasies of patients and, specifically, neurotic behavior. It is the assumption of psychoanalysis that an individual lives in a world of his own perception, deviating from such actuality as may exist through the distortion imposed by his own personal experience. Our past is the lens through which we observe the present. In the symptoms of neurosis, one sees an actual regression of behavior into the protective illusions of the past. If one examines an obsessional neurosis, or simply the obsessional behavior in which most of us indulge from time to time, it is amazing how much these relate to the rewarded behaviors of childhood. We tend to be obsessive about cleanliness, bowel habits, straightening, tidying, waking and bedding activities. In the obsessive's behavior we so often see those qualities which were deemed "good" in the child by parental standards. The least compulsive of us tend to be most compulsive in precisely those areas of behavior that dominated the first few years of life and earned the accolade, "That's a good boy (or girl)." In our eating patterns, in our excreting patterns, in our dressing, and in our bedtime rituals, we are guaranteeing our security by ritually impressing our internalized parents with our goodness and obedience.

A similar link to childhood definitions of security through dependence can be extrapolated by examining the behavior involved in phobias. At one time it was fashionable to have a distinct, separate interpretation of each individual phobia; fear of heights always meant x and fear of crowds, y. We tend now to see more the common thread that binds this diverse symptomatology into a consistent pattern. Many phobias seem to involve a concept of entrapment: elevators, subways, tunnels, airplanes, bridges, situations in which there seems no way out. If one examines the development of a classic travel phobia, the individual will feel safe traveling except through these previously mentioned specific terrifying situations. Gradually with the typical extending phobia, it will go beyond the subway and elevator. The first extension will be overnight trips; the individual will begin to limit these, and slowly he will begin to avoid superhighways as distinguished from local roads. Careful questioning will make it apparent that the superhighway, because of its limited access and egress, implies again a kind of entrapment not unlike a tunnel or bridge. Some phobics know the precise distance between each set of exits on a turnpike and can travel those roads in the areas where those exits are within a few miles. Eventually the travel becomes progressively more limited, and the distance from home deemed safe begins to shrink.

When one examines such "no way out" situations, at first they seem to be situations of danger, e.g., the airplane or subway, but one also notices that the same panic exists, often in the same people, in such seemingly non-threatening environments as barbershops. This has often been attributed to the presence of a man with a straight razor or scissors, which may contribute in part to certain phobic responses. It is also the ludicrous position of being half-lathered, or half-shaved, or wet-haired, and, indeed, women under dryers will experience the same sense of entrapment. Careful examination then reveals that in many of these patients it is also the sense of "no way out." More exactly, one should say, "no way home." The same anxiety exists for phobics at a formal dinner as distinguished from informal restaurant dining; in a large auditorium in the central seats where absences would be conspicuous, as distinguished from the aisle seats. At any public performance, if one wishes to detect a population with a high incidence of phobias, one would be wise to select all aisle seats, back rows, easy access to exit locations.

Phobics can be seen, across the specific symbols of their individual symptoms, to share a common terror—namely, separation from home. The phobic is distressingly similar to that two-year-old separated from his mother in a crowd. Safety here is visualized, if not in the parents, at least in the tangible symbolic aspects residual to them. The individual who despairs of his own capacity for coping regresses to the earliest mechanism of adaptation, dependency. He recalls a time when he was safe because he was loved. Most of us, at least at the earliest stages of our life, have experienced some caring and some loving, and even this small residue may be used to build an illusion of safety.

After all of this, I am not suggesting that we are not capable of destroying the loving aspects of our nature and removing them from the natural order of transmissible traits. We have already seen significant erosions of it—the helpless child may elicit a response, but the helpless individual on the street no longer seems to. The callousness of the social culture of the city has been well documented, witness the adolescent who kills an elderly woman because she is an easy victim and killing facilitates his aims. The inability of so many to identify with the aged, who surely represent to anyone of sense a vision of his own personal future, is a distressing sign. It is ironic that René Dubos should document his case for the goodness of man in the discovery of a prehistoric skeleton of a congenitally crippled and blind being of an older age. The implication is obvious: even before the time of civilization and culture, there existed a caring sense in Homo sapiens which allowed for the nourishment and sustenance into old age of a helpless member of the human race, unlike other animals which leave their maimed behind.

One psychoanalyst who has significantly attended to the concept of love, Erich Fromm, presumes that we have already lost the natural capacity. He pessimistically discusses love in terms of an animal who no longer has the impulse, but must learn it as an art. What *was* instinctual is instinctual no more. Fromm looks at love not as a label descriptive of the relationship between one and a loved object, but rather only as a modality used in dealing with isolation. "The basis for our need to love lies in the experience of separateness and the resulting need to overcome the anxiety of separateness by the experience of union." He divides love into various categories, the last of which is self-love. The fact that he spends as much time discussing this concept as the other four put together is a clear indication of Fromm's emphasis.

We, of course, are capable of changing even our better nature. Such determinants are never more than potentials with extraordinary capacity for modification by experience. In order for each successive generation to fulfill its potential for becoming caring individuals, they must be treated in a caring way. We must be made to feel lovable in order to be loving. The degree to which we are nurtured and cared for will inevitably determine the degree to which we will be capable of nurturing and caring.

Dependency is being given only a cursory examination here, although it surely demands a fuller one, because in this book it is to be used as a portal leading to the equally important concept of the caring nature of people. A loving nature in the adult must be built early in infancy; it is in the crucial relationships of the first years of life that our self-image is forged, and it is here that our capacities to relate are either nurtured or destroyed. The nature of the influences from mother to child are therefore essential. The kind of nurturing and loving that adults give to these developing creatures will determine that which they in turn will pass on to the following generation. It is crucial therefore to examine the nature of nurture itself. For this nurturing supplies the stuff on which is built personhood, as well as person. Proper nurture will guarantee the development not just of an adult, but of a caring adult.

CHAPTER IV

The Nature of Nurture: Food and More

Early infancy is the crucible and forge in which the potential of an animal is molded and shaped into the model of its kind—or damaged or destroyed. The neonate is "in process" in a way that the human being is at no other time of its post-natal existence.

Despite the fact that adults often know better intellectually, there is an inevitable emotional tendency to view the newborn infant as a miniature adult, at least on the physical level. But the newborn infant is no more a tiny adult physically than he is mentally or socially. He is an incomplete adult. Those adorable little wrists that are so appealing to doting parents are not wrists at all. They represent absences —the wristbones are not present at birth. The complete pattern of eight wristbones will not be fully present until the child is close to five years of age. Similarly, crucial parts of the nervous system are not yet completed at birth. The child is incapable of performing certain activities because he simply does not have the equipment to do so. In addition, many of the developed parts of the neonate which are actually present are in a state of extreme and delicate vulnerability, dependent on the proper environment in order to mature and develop; with an inappropriate environment they will atrophy and be destroyed.

Early imprinting is crucial for almost all animals, and has been dealt with extensively in the literature of ethology. By this time everyone must be aware of the quaint and pathetic capacity of a small duckling to follow the first moving object to cross its visual screen in the critical period, whether it be a piece of mechanical machinery such as a tractor, or a dog, or indeed a human being. Beyond imprinting are examples of critical environmental factors if normal systems are to mature. If, for instance, the infant cat is deprived of visual stimulation in the first days of life, he will never develop vision, but will remain blind for the rest of his life. This is not merely, as had been previously assumed, due to the lack of development of visual perception; recent work has indicated that with the deprivation of visual stimuli after birth, the visual cortex of the brain either fails to develop or, if present at birth, goes into attrition. There is an actual organic failure. In order for the visual cortex to develop after birth, there must be exposure to visual stimuli. It is not therefore just psychological or physiological functioning, but physical development that can be damaged by early deprivation.

Numerous experiments on all sorts of animals, from lower mammals to higher ones, have demonstrated that various deprivations early in life can alter the capacity of the animal for higher functions; interfere with its taking its social place; affect its capacity for cognition and learning; destroy the development of a sexual life; diminish the range of activity and playing; and inhibit normal emotionalism. We must no longer think merely in terms of the individual and his environment; we must introduce a third set of variables. The problems of development are related to the individual, his environment, and timing. Certain environmental influences must be produced at a critical period or they might just as well not be introduced at all. Obviously, in the example of light deprivation, no amount of exposure to a world of sunshine could compensate for that early deprivation.

At this point it should be obvious that what is true of the lower animals is true to an extraordinary degree of man as well. The newborn infant particularly requires specific treatments in order to thrive, because it is still, in essence, an extra-uterine fetus undergoing rapid growth and development. If certain factors are withheld, it will die; withholding others will stunt physical development. Because of the enormously rapid, intense, and concentrated growth and development of the brain in the first year of life, those specifically human functions focused in brain activity are particularly vulnerable. There are crucial factors that are essential for the infant's emotional and psychological growth; if sufficient of these are withheld, what develops will be a human being only in form and not in the substance that dignifies humanity. These varied requisites for normal development can be collectively designated "nurture."

Traditionally, early infancy has been seen as being dominated by the feeding situation. The child at the breast is the universal symbol of infancy. So profound is the importance of the early feeding relationship that it was given exclusive sovereignty in the traditional Freudian literature. This early period was referred to as the oral stage, and most of psychoanalysis devotes its attention to the oral needs of the child in the first year of life. Certainly they are overwhelming and crucial; and the equation of nurture and feeding is a dominant one.

Freud tended to visualize all development as the evolution of the sexual constitution and the sexual instinct proceeding from that first oral stage. This was not as constricting a focus as it might seem, for, in the process of so doing, Freud began to expand sexuality until it included in essence all pleasure functions and all motive drives. In *Three Essays on the Theory of Sexuality*, the critical watershed paper, he developed a concept of the ontogenesis of the sexual instinct, describing the first period of childhood as the oral stage. He commented that the first and most important activity in the child's life was sucking at the mother's breast. This is seen as a function of the most basic self-preservative drive, since food is a base-line necessity for survival. He observed that the child not only gets food but, in addition, pleasure. He defined the pleasure as being experienced in the mouth and lips of the child, and called this oral pleasure, and he described this period as one of oral eroticism.

It must be understood that, in the Freudian scheme, early childhood is seen as a period in which there are diffuse sexual urges, not yet dominated or integrated into a drive for sexual union. Indeed, the sexual aims of the child are not focused on external objects at all but rather on parts of its own body. It is not until four or five years of age that the child will fuse these diverse elements of sexuality and begin to focus on objects outside himself.

Freud was a superb clinical observer, and while we may now reject much of the theoretical structure he imposed on his clinical observation, the observations themselves have not been found faulty. He noticed that after the child was taken off the breast, it continued to desire the sucking pleasure it had lost, and often would then turn to its own body, particularly at this stage by sucking its thumb. This sucking seemed to be independent of the need of nourishment, for even a well-fed baby would indulge in the activity. Freud therefore postulated that there was a kind of innate pleasure-sucking, independent of ingestion.

What Freud did in his hypothesis was to present a reasonable link between the survival needs of the child and its pleasure needs expressed through the oral processes. That these are crucial links can be confirmed by any individual's merely looking into his own past or current behavior.

The feeding process is the primary event in both the biological existence of the child and its psychological and so-

cial life. It is the primary factor in the communication between the infant and that person who, he quickly learns,
supports his life style as well as his life. There develops, therefore, a fusion and confusion between food and security that
is to last throughout life.

It is now fashionable to state that we are what we eat.
But what we eat in early life is predictable and relatively
constant (except in extreme deprivation) and is therefore
less important than the process and milieu of eating. In this
sense, as in restaurant ratings, the stars for "ambiance" may
be more relevant than the rating for "food quality." The
literature relating to food, eating, and security is so massive
and so convincing, and has made such a conclusive case for
the fusion of food and security, that it has become part of
popular culture and common recognition. Personal self-
observation readily confirms the confusion and fusion. Almost every individual has had the experience of walking to
a well-stocked refrigerator wanting "something." In that refrigerator might be an example of every possible taste sensation: roast beef, cheese, pickles, jam, peanut butter, milk,
beer, fruit, etc. The bored, tired, or anxious person opens
the refrigerator and finds "nothing appealing." Obviously
what has happened is that the individual wants something
"nourishing," but nourishment may mean love, affection,
companionship, entertainment, or sex, and the average refrigerator is ill equipped in these areas. He misreads his
hunger for "something" as the primary hunger for food.

Eating is not the only activity pressed into serving security.
It is not uncommon to hear from men (and now progressively
more often from women) of college age descriptions of the
build-up of tensions while studying before an examination,
in which the question of whether to relieve the tension by
eating something or by masturbating arises as almost an
alternative decision. The anxious individual may feel free
to do both and still remain anxious. Masturbation at such
time is not a response to sexual stimulation at all. The

masturbation is the same kind of reassurance that eating is, merely derived from a later stage of development. The desire to masturbate in this case precedes sexual excitement, and the latter must be generated (and often cannot be) to permit the act which here clearly serves security rather than pleasure. Masturbation, like eating, often serves nonsexual needs in a variety of situations. It is unquestionably the most widely used effective non-prescriptive soporific.

Oral substitutes for security are even more direct and primitive (earlier) than sexual substitutes. They are more common and diverse. Dreams of patients in analysis abound with restaurants, bakeries, and candy stores, with the analyst / parent as the provender-provider. Also certain foods hold a special position in serving more specific purposes. An individual who is quite sated may still have a desire for something sweet, as a specifically defined self-reward, or even perhaps a forbidden fruit.

A not uncommon sign of anxiety is a compulsive swallowing; this can be extended into a *globus hystericus*—the panicky feeling that one cannot swallow. Of course there are those who carry swallowing beyond this into compulsive eating, and massive obesity results. This is not to suggest that obesity rests solely on this mechanism; more complete studies indicate numbers of reasons. There is, after all, more to the meaning of fatness than just the matter of the ingestion that leads to it—for example, isolation, expansion of size, protection from sexual attention, a wall of insulation. Inevitably, however, one of the factors is the symbolic self-reward or self-love that is characterized by continuous feeding.

To appreciate the oral bind on us, to sense the non-nutritive aspects of orality, one has only to examine the amount of human irrationality that involves sticking things in one's mouth. With all our concern for improvement of health care, we extend ourselves precious little. We passively await health as though it were a gift from "Daddy." We ignore all those factors which we could control. A cure for cancer would probably increase average life expectancy less than alteration of man's oral incorporative tendencies. If we would only eat less of the wrong things, or simply eat less, we would be less vulnerable to coronary artery disease.

The compulsive urge to stick something in our mouths, to replicate the early feeding situation, has no better example than in the smoking pattern that dominates our culture. Despite repeated evidence, increasingly clear, that man reduces his opportunity for a healthy old age by inhaling a cancer-producing product—cigarettes—we continue on a massive scale to inflict these internal wounds on ourselves. A government which will outlaw a drug remotely suggesting the possibility of producing skin cancer in a rat will timidly drag its feet in the face of the most important commercially disseminated poison. Paradoxically, this vestigial behavior left over from the sucking infant is often commercially sold to the gullible and susceptible adolescent boy as a sign of manhood and power. The cigarette, despite the advertisement, is not a phallic augmentation; it is, rather, an adult pacifier.

Two more detailed examples may better dramatize the meaning of "orality," or the fusion of the idea of oral pleasure with love, security, and a multitude of other factors—the non-nutritive aspects of eating. The first example is the disease called peptic ulcer. A peptic ulcer, on the simplest level, is an erosion of the lining of the stomach, or more commonly of the duodenal portion of the intestines. This erosion or ulceration can lead to bleeding, perforation, and death, either through contamination of the abdominal cavity or hemorrhaging. It is a serious condition. Yet the ulcer patient is often a subject of humor and jokes, probably because of an early intuitive recognition (even before the development of psychosomatic medicine) of the strong relationship between digestive processes and emotions. "You're giving me an ulcer" as an expression carries all the meanings of frustration, anger, anxiety, and irritation that one tends to find in an ulcer patient.

The ulceration is due to a combination of chemical and physical factors, central to which is the fact that in the ulcer patient the stomach seems to be constantly prepared for the ingestion of food. There is hyperactivity and motility of the stomach wall and with it a hypersecretion of gastric juices and hydrochloric acid. When the person is not actually eating, this constant readiness, or "desire," to eat allows the secretions to occur in an empty stomach and literally digest their own stomach wall.

Very early in the developing field of psychosomatic medicine, peptic ulcer became a chief target of inquiry; a remarkable unanimity on the nature of "ulcer type" exists among diverse researchers in this field. Allowing for the differences in technical language of the various investigators, they all concur in defining the ulcer type as likely to be an aggressive, self-sufficient, successful individual who denies himself all dependency gratifications. He is an individual who externally insists on being self-sufficient, and is always prepared to be a parental figure, while underneath he is hungry for caring, loving, and a dependency role.

It is interesting to observe what has evolved as the ideal treatment for an ulcer patient. First, he was put into a hospital—often against his wishes. Once there, despite the grousing, he seemed to relish the situation. There is no more infantilizing position than that of a hospital patient. In many ways it is an experience of absolute indignity, and were it not under the benevolent model of a therapeutic process, would not be tolerated by society. When you are admitted to a hospital, you are immediately divested of your clothes and given an uncomfortable garment, sure to offend whatever modesty you have by exposing your vital parts in the most embarrassing positions. It is usually fastened with the ties one associates with infants' clothing, where buttons are a nuisance and zippers may be harmful. You are told when you can eat and what you can eat. You are told when you must go to bed and when you must get up. You are told who may visit you, when they may visit you, and how long they may stay. Lights are out at a specific hour and your entertainments are restricted to those allowable by the authorities. If you have, heaven help you, an "interesting" disease, all sorts of strangers will feel free to insert every conceivable kind of protuberance into every available orifice of your body. Your doctor will refer to you by first name or patronizing euphemisms while you will always respectfully refer to him as Dr. Krankheit. Your chart, which contains all the crucial data that would seem to be of interest to you more assuredly than to anybody else, will lie at the foot of your bed, and were you to dare reach for it, you would be figuratively hand-slapped, like a child reaching for some forbidden gratification.

Some of this is necessary for the health of the patient, and even more for the convenience of the hospital; yet all of it is endured, yes, even embraced, by a patient terrified at the prospect of death and illness and ready to ingratiate those who are vested with the power of health. On this treatment the ulcer patient thrives, particularly when for his special benefit an additional therapeutic maneuver is added. The traditional treatment, in the early days of psychosomatic medicine, and it was effective, was to put the patient on a Sippy diet. This diet consisted of no solids but rather a substitution of a formula of half milk and half cream to be given 2 to 4 ounces at a time every two to four hours. Indeed, in severe cases a tube was placed in the stomach so there was a constant drip of nourishment into the patient.

Many modifications have since evolved, but tender loving care has always been an essential feature of treating ulcer patients. The enforcement of the dependency state, which they crave unconsciously yet consciously cannot ask for, is usually an essential ingredient of any program.

The lesson is that security and peace were at their maximum—or seemed so—in infancy. The most important physical need for the infant is that of food. His behavior is motivated primarily by the subjective awareness of that hunger and thirst, and the cycle of hunger, ingestion, satiation will fill the greater part of an infant's day. The behavior patterns evolved during this oral period represent much of the early adaptation of the organism, and as such are indelible. They exist imprinted on the individual and are available for potential revivability whenever future need may arise. In the unconscious mind of the adult, dependency —in terms of both helplessness and being cared for—is associated with the original experience of infant-feeding. When the adult feels threatened or frightened and incapable of coping, he will fall back on the specific technique of a dependency adaptation, and more often than not he will symbolize it in terms of being fed.

Another dramatic example of the fusion of dependency, security, and love is seen in the varied meanings of the fellatio fantasy and often determines its role and priority in lovemaking. In one of his first elaborated cases (1905), Freud discussed certain oral symptoms of his young patient, Dora, and related this to a fellatio fantasy. Since then, it has been recognized that fellatio is an opportunity for sexual enjoyment which at the same time seems to replicate a feeding situation.

It has long been noted that in the sexual behavior of certain homosexuals, where fellatio plays a more important part than in most heterosexual activity, the sexual activity differs from heterosexuality in many ways beyond the gender subject chosen. When a heterosexual is told that he cannot have sexual activity, for the most part there is merely a feeling of deprivation, and he will resort to alternatives such as masturbation. This was not atypical during a period when fidelity was a relatively common ideal. When the homosexual is deprived of sexual activity, there is more often an obsessive build-up of tension, and one more often recognizes the homo-sexual act as obsessionally driven than the heterosexual act. The deprived homosexual tends to respond in the same way as a cigarette smoker who is deprived of a cigarette or an obese patient who is deprived of his food. For these individuals, the homosexual act stands for more than just the release of sexual tension or a means of lovemaking. It has the compulsive meaning of a security symbol.

It is true that certain kinds of heterosexuality are also obsessively driven, and there are classic Don Juans who are driven to repeated pleasureless acts which afford only the relief of satisfying a compulsion. But in analysis of homosexual fantasies, it becomes especially apparent that the behavior often is as richly endowed with nonsexual meanings as sexual meanings. Lionel Ovesey has used the word "pseudohomosexuality" to describe homosexual activity in homosexuals (or homosexual fantasies in heterosexuals) the primary function of which is other than sexual. In his description he sees two other functions as being crucial: first is the power struggle, in which the act of fellatio may be envisioned as a submission to or a disarming of a potential attacker; second is the other sense of disarming—it is an ingratiation of a potential parent, and therefore an act of dependency.

In analyzing fantasies involving fellatio, abundant evidence emerges that the sucking of the penis can be seen as a restitution of the primary situation at the breast. For those who are limited to achieving sexual pleasure exclusively through performing fellatio, the act reassures while allowing pleasure. Whatever anxiety exists in the concept of the sexual act for these individuals is alleviated by fusing it with the reassurance of that primal scene of comfort.

So powerful was the case that Freud made for orality and the resonance it achieved in personal experience that it became the central thesis of child development even beyond the psychoanalytic framework. Before 1958, both psychoanalysts and learning theorists conceptualized the primary bond between the mother and her infant as being rooted almost completely in the feeding situation. Yet the feeding situation is more than the squirting of nutrients into a gastro-intestinal tract, particularly in the traditional breast feeding, but certainly also in the bottle feeding that simulates it. It is a situation of embrace, pressure, contact, flesh-to-flesh engagement, fondling, cooing, tickling, talking, stroking, squeezing; it is the warmth of the body, the pulsation of the mother's heart, the brushing of her lips, and the smell of her secretions.

All of this was of course recognized; but the tendency, and a logical one at that, was to think that these latter activities *became* pleasurable by virtue of their association with feeding. This interpretation fits well into the framework of the primary-drive-based conceptualizations which were popular at the time in almost all psychologies. In the natural environment it is enormously difficult to separate the multiple variables, and the satisfaction of physiological needs such as hunger is not readily teased apart from the giving of contact and stimulation.

Pathologists had long noted that, in the animal kingdom, the grooming contact between the mother and offspring was not as random as had been formerly thought and was not simply a matter of poking, nuzzling, or licking indiscriminately. Nor was it merely a matter of affection. The licking and nuzzling movements of the mother are often essential to initiate activity of primary importance in the young. It was discovered that particularly without the perianal licking of the parent, it is quite possible for the young mammal—dog or cat, for example—to be incapable of urinating, and because of such urinary retention to die. The licking contact and stimulation are essential physiological ingredients to initiate the complex processes of evacuation. Skin contact, proprioceptive contact, nuzzling, may therefore be as crucial a part of the nurture transmitted from the mother to the child as the food.

In 1958, John Bowlby, an English psychiatrist, began to speculate about the possible significance of similar behavior in encouraging attachment between the mother and child. The concept of "attachment" that evolved has altered the thinking of most dynamic developmentalists. Bowlby was a part of the psychoanalytic community and was capable of making the leap from the data of ethology to the hypotheses that were rooted in his psychoanalytic insights and the general psychoanalytic tradition.

There are limitations to what human experimentation will allow. The natural situation, particularly between human mother and child, is complex and crucial, and one controls variables only with serious moral and ethical risks. Bowlby had the advantage of an artificial research population in those children separated from their mothers to protect them from the London blitz during World War II. However, direct control and observation of infants was still limited and difficult. Further, it was difficult in the beginning to know which essential ingredients should be examined or controlled. The natural situation, where the mother feeds at the same time that she fondles, talks to, and caresses her child, does not lend itself to isolating the impact of the various ingredients. One could not tell what was due to the satisfaction of the hungers, or separate this from the giving of contact and stimulation. In one of the serendipitous occurrences of research, H. F. Harlow, an animal psychologist, had begun, coincident with Bowlby, his now famous studies of the relationships of infant monkeys to artificial surrogates. Among many other controlled studies one in particular was startling. He divided the functions of mothering for a group of infant monkeys into two incomplete artificial mothers. One of them supplied nourishment in the sense of food, but was a cold, non-tactile, wire-mesh machine; at the same time there was present a warm, soft, terrycloth "mother" which supplied no nutrients (i.e., food) at all. The studies demonstrated that the infant monkeys raised by these artificial surrogates

invariably preferred (loved?) the warm and soft cloth
mothers, despite the fact that they received no nourishment
from them but got all of their life-sustaining food from the
wire-mesh mother. It was with the terrycloth mother that the
infants chose to spend most of their time, clinging fiercely—
possessive and desiring by every observable standard. As
startling, however, was the fact that when exposed to any
threat—an artificially created danger or potentially dangerous
situation—it was to this terrycloth mother that the infant
monkeys retreated for reassurance.

In later studies, Harlow and some of his colleagues demonstrated the profound influence of withdrawing all social,
tender, and loving contacts with one's own kind. They
established experimental situations in which all the presumed
ingredients for physiological development were supplied
(nourishment, water, proper temperature, protection against
diseases, etc.) and all that was missing was contact with a
parent figure. In these studies it was shown that the deprived
creatures were almost unidentifiable as being "of their own
kind" in terms of their social behavior. They had lost their
"humanness," we would say if they were children. Anyone, regardless of how unsophisticated as to psychology or
ethology, who has walked through a laboratory and seen
some of these strange creatures, recognizes immediately something terribly disturbed in their attitudes. They indulge in
odd, isolated, autistic behavior of the kind one sees in neglected, backward patients or the most severely retarded.
They don't seem real or alive. These animals were raised
with the best surrogate (the cloth one); while this surrogate
gives some contact comfort, and, as we have seen, is better
than the wire-mesh feeding machine, what it gives is in-
sufficient to guarantee the development of a normal adult.
These conditions allow for the survival of the infant to
adulthood, but produce an adult that cannot interrelate
with its kind and cannot sexually reproduce.

The studies showed further that the effect of isolation

depended in great part on the time and duration of the contact deprivation. Up to three months of deprivation seemed in these animals to allow a certain reversibility; but animals isolated beyond that point, even for a period as short as six months, seemed permanently endangered.

The animals were deficient in precisely those features which are most closely associated in the human animal with his humanness: the capacity to enjoy the company of others, to relate socially and sexually, to become a member of a social unit, to have "emotions," to be able to play and to learn. It is difficult to know what the specific deficiencies are of the cloth surrogate, but obviously it is the whole complex interrelationship—the give and take of talk and touch, of feeding and fondling, of loving and caring—that produces infants who will later emerge into adults capable of assuming that same role with their own children.

Harry Stack Sullivan was one of the few psychoanalysts who adequately appreciated the complexity of contact. His interpersonal theories were directed toward relationships and social living rather than internal mechanisms. He used the simple word "tenderness" to describe this complex amalgam of caring contact; it is not surprising, therefore, that he would also recognize, well before the classical psychoanalytic community, the importance of identification and emotional learning beyond the first few years.

Later research has shown that with monkeys, at least, some reversibility is possible, but only with great effort. Also it has emerged that the opportunity merely to *observe* caring behavior can be, at least in part, a substitute for the opportunity to participate in social activity.

All of this work gave new impetus to the observation of psychoanalytic writers who were becoming increasingly aware that institutionalized babies, even in the best of institutions, seem to lack a capacity for affection, warmth, and human contact possessed by infants raised even in inadequate homes where there may be fear, or deprivation of a physical sort, but where contact is frequent. This observation has become a strong impetus for either the reduction of institutionalization or changes in institutional procedures, and the lowering of standards, if necessary, for foster care to provide early infants with a perhaps less generous material existence in exchange for a more giving emotional environment. The deprivations of the first year of life seem almost calculated to be tit for tat; retaliation in kind. For children raised in institutions and deprived of social contact have the greatest deficiencies in the capacities for loving, giving, altruistic behavior, conscience, and social responsibility. Early deprivation of such socialization is considered one of the strongest factors responsible for the unfeeling, conscienceless individual known as a psychopath.

Interestingly, a careful analysis of the various forms of attention and contact offered children—holding, playing, talking to, and so on—leads to the conclusion that the *kind* of contact is less important than the *amount*. Even when the mother was only the provider of stimulation (giving toys, etc.), it served the need for social contact. She did not need to play with them, merely to be there.

Intriguing studies, again drawn from animals, this time sheep and goats, demonstrated the unbelievable reciprocity of these relationships between parent and offspring. It has been described how contact with the mother was necessary for the development of a certain kind of child. These studies showed that mothering on the part of the mature animal was not in itself an independent or automatic function but also was dependent on intimate contact with the infant. While there is variability between species (and even within the species), a clear-cut pattern emerges. If the mother were allowed to maintain contact for a matter of the first few days with her infant, and then separated from it, she would invariably return to her nurturing role upon the return of the infant. She would do so only on the presentation of her own infant, rejecting, butting, even kicking to death a strange one. If she is allowed to remain in the presence of her infant for only a few hours, and then separated, sufficient inducement for mothering will occur but it will be erratic. She seems incapable of distinguishing her infant from others; she will indiscriminately accept and nurture any young. If she is deprived of her child immediately, postpartum, she will reject, butt, or kick her own as well as a strange infant.

It seems, then, that the presence of the infant is essential to trigger the very mothering response in the adult that is essential for the infant's own survival and development! Drawing on this information, Klaus and his group, in 1970, cognizant of the separation of mothers and infants necessitated by a premature birth, wondered whether it is possible that in first mothers, these separations might indeed inhibit normal mothering responses. In other words, they wondered whether there were species-specific responses in the human animal as there were in others. And indeed they found there were:

> Observations in human mothers suggest that affectionate bonds are forming before delivery, but that they are fragile and may easily be altered in the first days of life. A preliminary inspection of fragments of available data suggests that maternal behavior may be altered in some women by a period of separation just as infant behavior is affected by isolation from the mother.

This, then, makes attachment not the passive clinging of one to another, not a parasitic, but rather a symbiotic model of mutual influence and nourishment, where giving and taking are indistinguishable, in a joyous and nourishing fusion that is certainly one model of love. The newborn infant, therefore, helpless as he may be, is not at the mercy of a chance response. It would seem that the very fact of his helplessness and the physical contact essential for the birthing and early feeding situations will, if unimpeded, stimulate certain stroking, caressing, and attendant responses in the parent which reciprocally and wonderfully are the necessities for his survival as a human being. Survival itself requires feeding, but feeding alone only guarantees the survival of something, not necessarily a person. For a full development into personhood, with sensitivities and sensibilities, with capacities to communicate and relate, a broader sense of nurture is necessary. It is necessary to be loved in a specific, caring way; it is being loved in this way that initiates in the child the capacity to give love to others.

Caring, of course, is not just a function of the mother-child relationship. Caring—that is, the protective, parental, tender aspects of loving—is a part of relationship among peers, child to parent, friend to friend, lover to lover, person to animal, and multiple other patterns. The fact that in this book I attend almost exclusively to the parent-child aspect of caring is because it is the essential paradigm whose presence is necessary for the diffusion of this human quality into the other aspects and relationships of life.

Even with severe deprivations, something of the child will survive. How "human" that something will be will to a tremendous extent depend on the nature of the nurture provided to the developing human being. As light and visual stimulation are essential for the development of the capacity to see, so to be cared for is essential for the capacity to be caring. And to be cared for refers to all aspects of that word: to be taken care of, to be concerned about, to be worried over, to be supervised, to be attended to—to be loved. patronized.

CHAPTER V

Attachment

In *The Symposium*, Plato devotes himself to an exploration of the nature of love. Along the way to his final enunciation of that idealized love that he was to call Eros, and which stands as an antithesis of the eros which was to dominate the Freudian mind, Socrates dismisses a number of theories of love in his search for *the* theory of love. Today we are not inclined to seek the definition of love, but *a* definition of loving. Love is seen to be so complex a matter that, if it is a unity, the substantive element of it is only understandable by analysis of its variable modes of expression. Among those theories abandoned by Socrates along the road to truth was the myth of Aristophanes. To me, this is the ultimate parable of caring and its relationship to future love. It is a prototype of the kind of attachment identification and fusion that is part of the process of *learning* to become a loving individual by being *cared for* by a loving individual. In abbreviated form, the myth is as follows:

> . . . first let me treat of the nature and state of man; for the original human nature was not like the present, but different. . . . The primeval man was round and had four hands and four feet, back and sides forming a circle, one head with two faces, looking opposite ways, set on a round neck and precisely alike; also four ears, two privy members, and the remainder to correspond. . . . Terrible was their might and strength, and the thoughts of their hearts were great, and they made an attack upon the gods. . . . The gods could not suffer their insolence to be unrestrained.

. . . At last, after a good deal of reflection, Zeus discovered a way. . . . "They shall continue to exist but I will cut them in two and then they will be diminished in strength and increased in numbers." He spoke and cut them in two . . . as you might divide an egg with a hair. . . .

Each of us when separated is but the indenture of a man, having one side only like a flat fish, and he was always looking for his other half. . . . And when one of them finds his other half . . . the pair are lost in an amazement of love and friendship and intimacy, and one would not be out of the other's sight, as I may say, even for a moment; these are they who passed their lives with one another; yet they could not explain what they desire of one another. For the intense yearning which each of them has towards the other does not appear to be the desire of intercourse, but of something else which the soul desires and cannot tell, and of which she only has a dark and doubtful presentment. Suppose Hephaestus . . . come to the pair who are lying side by side and say to them, "What do you people want of one another . . . do you desire to *be* wholly one? For if this is what you desire, I am ready to melt you into one and let you grow together. . . ." There is not a man among them when he heard this who would deny or who would not acknowledge that this meeting and melting in one another's arms, this becoming one instead of two, was the very expression of his ancient need. *And the reason is that human nature was originally one and we were whole, and the desire and pursuit of that whole is called love.*

So, too, in the development of the individual there is a peculiar pattern of original fusion, as in the early symbiotic relationship, followed by separation and refusion again in love. This is the normal order of development of loving in the human species. The first step in this sequence is the attachment of the child to the mother. Of course, what is being referred to as "attachment" here is more accurately a reattachment. After all, the child is literally attached to the mother in the first nine months of the fetal period via the umbilicus. This attachment is prematurely interrupted by birth. Birth, however, is not the end of the fetal period in the human being. It is merely an alteration of the arrangement, necessitated by the specific anatomy of the human child and mother.

As we have seen, there are other mammalian forms in which fetalization is divided into stages; specifically, the marsupials. The kangaroo gives birth to an incredibly small infant, which then ascends vertically from the birth canal into an externalized pouch on the mother. Once tumbling inside, it firmly attaches its mouth to a nipple and continues an almost direct anatomical attachment that seems incredibly parallel to the intra-uterine umbilical attachment. Here the tiny creature will continue to grow increasingly rapidly until it is prepared to make small forays out of the maternal pouch. This pouch, then, is a state of existence, half-internal and half-external, which continues the symbiosis of mother and child while allowing for the gradual exploration of the environment that will lead eventually to a mature, independent adult. The pouch is available to the developing young kangaroo even when it becomes absurdly (to the outside observer at least) mature in form. To see one of these young baby kangaroos leap into its mother's pouch, thereupon to be embraced by its folds, is a delight and astonishment to the uninitiated observer.

The human mother is endowed with no such pouch, her baby is less genetically fixed, and the lessons it must learn are incredibly more complex. What substitutes for the pouch is an environment, a milieu dominated by the caring psychology of the parent built on the intuitive emotional, and intellectually designed cultural, supports which preserve and protect the helpless creature. It is interesting to note that in most simple cultures the first design for supporting an infant is an artifact not at all unlike the marsupial pouch. The slings in which children are carried in most simple cultures ensure a physical attachment that almost inevitably would lead to the other forms of attachment behavior so necessary for the developing child. The development of the baby carriage, however, allows for a distancing that has potential danger, and may be yet another example of progress creating choices where none formerly existed. The traditional, simple mechanisms seem to have a direct link to the genetic directives which give birth to them. The complicated mechanisms create greater convenience but at the same time offer choices that are not always beneficial, and where discriminating between good and bad may not be easy. The problems in development are insidious because the results of an improper environment may be evidenced in forms so different from the initiating cause; and cause and effect are always separated by a time lag that makes the recognition of their relationship enormously difficult.

This reattachment, then, that is called attachment, is absolutely essential for the nurture (in its broadest sense) required by that externalized fetus known as the human infant.

The language of attachment as distinguished from the traditional libido frame of reference has had many fortuitous effects on the study of early childhood development. In the traditional psychoanalytic framework, the examination of orality depends on inferential judgments about a child incapable of articulating, whose unconscious defenses could not be examined by traditional methods of free association or play. Attachment, as a concept drawn from ethology, focuses on the specific behavior and interrelationships and allows psychoanalytic inferences to be drawn *from* those behaviors. Unlike the behaviorists, who are prepared to see the individual as the sum total of his behavior, and are therefore free to ignore emotions and the internal life, the students of attachment see behavior as an index of the individual's innermost emotional life. But because they are describing behavior, a common ground has been established among behavioral psychologists, ethologists, psychoanalysts, neonatologists, learning theory experts, and educators.

One can view all attachment behavior as serving a single essential function: to facilitate "a proximity to mother as a predictable outcome," as Bowlby puts it, to bind the parent to the child, to make sure the mother stays close at hand. Crying, clinging, sucking, smiling, following, hailing, or calling by name, all can be described as attachment behavior because they serve to secure the presence of the mother. It must be understood that "presence" here has a very special meaning; as Bowlby points out, it does not necessarily refer to physical presence: "In reference to an attachment figure presence is to be understood as implying ready accessibility, rather than actual immediate presence."

In studies alluded to earlier, it was established that while the importance of food cannot be minimized, oral gratification is not a prerequisite for establishing an essential attachment. Something less concrete, something more romantic, seems to be the key factor. Something in the intensity of contact and the quality of care that is provided is almost more important than the ability of the mother to satisfy the survival needs of hunger and thirst. Sullivan's concept of "tenderness" evokes some, but not all, of this quality.

Under whatever mysterious influences the attachment takes place, once it does become established, the bond has a strength that is remarkably resistant to disruption. Attachment is a unique and strange phenomenon. It does not conform to traditional patterns of human behavior, but seems, rather, quite atypical in terms of the ways people normally learn and normally respond. It does not even follow the set patterns of conditioning. In the words of Robert Sears: "The seeming suddenness, intensity, ardor—even passion—and the prolonged irreversibility of the attachment responses are difficult to reconcile with the orderly progression of learning that characterizes such other action systems as attention seeking and achievement."

Anyone who has had a child is aware of the frantic, compelling quality of the baby's attention-seeking. And anyone who has had a child is also aware of how difficult it is to resist such appeals. It is this direct observation that has led to such strong support for an "innate bias for attachment." Most observers now feel that this is a propelled, natural, maturational development, as much a part of the genetic composition of the individual as growth of body parts and intellectual and emotional systems. These two, after all, can also be impeded and corrupted by an unsympathetic and unsatisfying environment.

What I am suggesting here is not the *tabula rasa* that certain behaviorists propose, but rather the recognition that there is an interaction between a natural direction and a sympathetic environment. Piaget, in his interactional theories, would seem sympathetic to this kind of view. In many ways it is much like Leibnitz's concept of "veined marble" rather than "clean slate." The baby is viewed as being born with a distinct, genetically defined potential, which will follow a relatively fixed course of development provided the genetic mechanism is allowed to operate. In order to do so, it requires the proper stimulation to activate its potential. If, at the maturationally appropriate time, the mother behaves in an appropriate way, attachment will occur.

The qualities that are required of a mother are interwoven in the nature, kind, frequency, and intensity of her actions toward her baby. Here what I am referring to are such actions as playing, feeding, talking, fondling, and so on. Something in the property of the stimulation is extremely important, something in the quality more than the kind. Obviously different cultures dictate different kinds of parental behavior to the child, different distributions, for example, between the amounts of time spent by a mother and father. Yet attachment can take place despite enormous disparities in the nature of the parental response to the identical entreaties and imprecations of the child. No, it is not the precise nature of what is done but something in the quality of the act that is the key ingredient.

But it is this quality of response that resists specific analysis. We know, for example, that infants exhibit an interest in human attributes over other stimuli of similar nature and intensity; a preferential response to the human voice and to the human face are among those that have been demonstrated. Babies prefer people to things or animals. In some studies it was shown that the intensity of the infant's attachment to its mother was proportional to the *speed* with which the person responded to the infant, as well as to the intensity of the interaction of the mother and child. How "ready" the parent is to comfort the child must be "interpreted" by the child as evidence of caring. Babies also seemed most securely attached and cried the least when their mothers were extremely responsive and spent large amounts of time with them. The preparedness of the mother to "give" to her child—whether measured in the immediacy of her response or in the amount of her attention and time—seems of prime importance.

While we do not begin to understand all of the ingredients that facilitate attachment, the mechanism certainly seems clear. In this area particularly, all capacities and all developing behavior must be seen as *neither* innate nor learned, but as a combination of the two. As in all of genetics, the nature/nurture distinction exists only in the degree to which capacities are environmentally stable or environmentally labile. Eye color is obviously an environmentally stable phenomenon. Height would have at one time been so considered, although recent experiences in changes of diet in the Japanese have shown the lability of even that function. More typically labile functions would be the potentials for artistic or athletic facility. In this sense these observations are consistent with modern theories of genetics.

The inordinately large number of environmentally labile behavior systems that characterize the human animal are both its strength and its weakness. Here, as everywhere else, the human being represents an extreme without competition in the animal kingdom. It is rendered particularly vulnerable to neglect since it has a minimum of fixed instinctual developments that progress independent of environment. This also, however, makes it the most proficient of animals in coping with extreme environmental variations. *Homo sapiens* is plastic and moldable, which means he is a learner *par excellence*.

One would normally think that attachment behavior would be classified among the particularly labile—vulnerable and sensitive to disruption. But in the case of the capacity for attachment, such behavior is remarkably stable, remarkably independent of environmental modification. "Indeed attachment behavior in the young, together with reciprocal parental care behavior, tend to be the most environmentally stable behaviors across species," according to Mary Ainsworth, the distinguished child development expert. In this sense it is much closer to eye color than to poetic imagination. As every practicing psychoanalyst has observed, what is remarkable in the human being is not his capacity to break down; it is his inordinate reserve of strength. Every symptom of neurosis is overdetermined; in other words, it must result from repeated assaults on integrity, multiple affronts to self-confidence.

Harry Harlow, in his pioneering study of mothering in primates, concluded that:

> The infant-mother affectional system is enormously powerful and probably less variable than any other of the functional systems. It is not surprising that this is so because strong infant-mother ties are essential to survival particularly in a

feral environment. The system is so binding that many infants can survive relatively ineffective mothering and the system will even continue with great strength in the face of strong and protracted punishment by unfeeling mothers.

That this is relatively stable does not mean that it is invulnerable to the cruelty of social institutions. The most heartbreaking evidence exists of infants who, because of the cruelly impersonal institutions in which they were forced to spend their early years, never developed the type of attachments that I have described. These infants, depending on the degree of deprivation, will either literally die because no one cares sufficiently for them to live; or they will survive as helpless autistic creatures; or they will enter into adult life emotionally and morally crippled, and as psychopaths will unconsciously and unwittingly wreak their vengeance on the society that has so terribly deprived them. Only the cruelest of institutions or parents would allow such neglect of children. The child, after all, makes his need known in the most compelling of fashions. And when deprived, it is touching to see the readiness with which children will accept alternatives or surrogates. Sometimes when no mother is present they may have the opportunity to form affectionate bonds with peers, and, when this occurs, they do so with an amazing intensity, as was demonstrated in the case of some World War II orphans.

Attachment behavior, once defined as such, is recognizable by every parent as part of his experience. At first it is crude, almost reflexive, in its manner; then as the baby matures, it begins to have a signaling quality about it and the parent begins to know the purposes of even these rudimentary actions. Characteristic of this is the example of an infant who will cry until his mother appears; as soon as he notices the mother, he stops crying; however, were she to begin to leave the room again, crying would resume. This obviously rudimentary means of communication is a means of signaling, or coercing, the mother—demanding that she stay near.

In this case it is clear that there is nothing specific the child wants (food, changing), merely the proximity of his mother.

As the child gets older, the need may be the same, but the behavior is subtler. One example reported the behavior of a two-year-old toddler who was intensely and busily exploring his environment. He seemed to be ignoring his mother, with only an occasional sidelong glance toward her—that is, as long as she was within the range of what he considered an acceptable distance from him. As soon as she stepped outside that range, he interrupted his explorations and actively set about reestablishing this acceptable distance. He did not require physical contact with the mother, only a fixed proximity. Physical contact only became necessary when the situation was charged with some potential danger, or seemed unfamiliar. Otherwise, the distance contact from the prescribed range was satisfactory. The acceptable range, i.e., the optimal distance, was variable, and dependent upon the child's comfort, his familiarity with his surroundings, and other changeable factors. Obviously the more comfortable and familiar the situation, the greater would be the distance that was found tolerable.

The need for attachment and the readiness to attach is so fundamental, so enormous, and, as we shall see later, so essential to the development of a truly independent but loving human being, that it will tolerate what, to the detached observer, seems the most inadequate of mothering behaviors. It is not weakened by brutal or even abusive behavior. Dorothy Burlingham and Anna Freud point out that: "Children will cling even to mothers who are continually cross and sometimes cruel to them. The attachment of a small child to his mother seems to a large degree independent of her personal qualities." And Harry Harlow comments: "The power, insistence and demandingness of the infant to make contact and the punishment the infant would accept would make strong men reach the point that they could hardly bear to observe this unmaternal behavior."

It is crucial to realize that when the baby begins to abandon attachment behavior, this does not in any way indicate a mitigating of his underlying affectionate feelings for the mother. The mother must not feel rejected or unloved. If anything, the early cessation of attachment behavior is a tribute to the effectiveness and the quality of the attachment. In order for proper development to occur, it is essential that the maturing child leave the mother's side more and more. It is the security that the earlier attachment gives to the child which allows him to attempt other equally important forms of behavior, such as active exploration of the environment. Obviously, the more secure the baby is in this early attachment, the freer he will be, the less he is likely to be constantly demanding the dependent ties to the parent.

As in other areas, so in attachment, the child learns with age the meaning of metaphor and the value of symbol. No longer is the concrete presence of the mother always needed, but her representations persist and are present in lingering attitudes and in reminiscences of care. When the child reaches the stage where his attachment can exist independent of actual manifestations of it in the proximity of the parent, the child is growing up—and growing up well.

This early attachment behavior transcends our concern for the welfare of any single infant during his first years; it is related to the adaptive purposes of the species. Obviously it calls for, and even triggers, protective parental responses which enhance the infant's survival opportunities. But it also is the first step in the development of loving relations among adults. Harry Stack Sullivan tell us: "Before speech is learned, every human being . . . has to learn certain gross patterns of relationship with the parent, or with someone who mothers him. These gross patterns become the utterly varied but quite firm foundations on which a great deal more is superimposed or built."

The attachment relationship is in many ways the foundation of all later affectionate or loving relationships, and is considered essential to form the more sophisticated, less instinctually bound, relationships of mature life. This first bond is overwhelmingly important in determining the capacity and the quality of all other later significant relationships.

The process of the infant's first attachments, surely not yet love, will determine the capacities to make identification, and these will facilitate mature love. This does not mean that the mechanisms are the same for all three, or that we form our later attachments on the model of the early one. In many ways, were we to form our later attachments on that model, it would imply a failure of the first attachment. No, the process of identification and loving is much different, but requires an independent and secure, a venturesome and self-confident individual, who will emerge only when early attachments have been facilitated.

It is generally accepted that attachment is the one kind of social interaction which each child must experience sometime during the first three years of life if development is to proceed relatively normally. Once the infant has attached to its mother, it is amazing how immediately and rapidly it is prepared to enter into a whole series of attachments to other figures. The infants who were not attached to their mothers or to any other primary caretakers are found not to attach to anyone else. Some maintain that if there are no attachments during infancy or early childhood, there will be no possibility of forming sound later relationships such as heterosexual love or love for one's children, and I believe this is correct.

It is in this context that the recent work with premature infants and their mothers has particular significance. Alerted to the importance of early contact from the study of attachment literature and ethology (remember the goats who rejected their young after separation), certain researchers recognized the potentially disastrous consequences of current hospital practice. If there is a critical postpartum period when the human mother is particularly sensitive to her child, and prepared for attachment, hospitals in the United States are frighteningly disrespectful of this. Current hospital practice, which separates mother and infant immediately after birth, would seem designed to disrupt the essential contact period necessary to allow the natural responses of mother to child to develop. In these terms, then, it would be crucially important to rethink and redesign our obstetrical services. We tend now to think of maternal and infant care as separate concerns, forgetting that the relationship, the infant-mother symbiosis, is something more than, and essential to, the well-being of the individual partners. Through a series of studies, Dr. Marshall Klaus (an authority on premature babies) and his colleagues have documented their firm belief that such an overhaul of current hospital practice is essential. In the human being, a disproportionate increase in "disorders of mothering" (including the ultimate "disorder," the death of the child) arises in situations associated with an early neonatal separation of mother and infant as, for example, in premature births. They conclude therefore that:

> There is a sensitive period in the human mother which is the optimal time for an affectionate bond to develop between the mother and her infant. The influence of mother-infant contact and interaction in the early minutes and hours after delivery on subsequent mothering behavior is supported by results of six of the eight controlled studies of mothers of premature infants and parents of full-term infants. The effects may persist in the mother of a full-term for as long as two years, affect the weight gain of her infant in the first month, and be manifest in the performance of the premature infants forty-two months later.

Before there was a psychology, we had intuitively known that how a mother treated her child would determine the kind of adult that child would become. Modern psychology emphasized that the way a mother treats a child in the first year of life is the crucial factor. But now the neonatologists are telling us that how the mother treats the child will itself be initiated and influenced by the child! It will be seriously affected by her opportunity for contact with the child in that first few days of life. Instinctive, reflexive maternal behavior, in order to be triggered, requires contact with the child. When it is triggered, it follows with an automaticity that extends beyond the first child into other childbearing experiences. Depriving a mother who has never had an experience with mothering of the presence of her child diminishes her capacity to offer a quality and quantity of caring behavior, which in turn may diminish the capacity for that child to develop into as affectionate, caring, and affectual person as it might have been. In that sense, then, the carriage and the crib, those currently universal symbols in the modern world of love and caring, may be agents of alienation— products of a technical age serving purposes antithetical to their intent.

The human infant, endowed with the massive brain that is the source of all technology, demands release from the maternal womb before it is prepared to face the outer world. In that womb, it was bound to the mother by that marvelous organ, half-mother, half-child, called the placenta; and through the placenta, all requisites for the infant's survival were automatically transmitted. That unified creature of Aristophanes existed in the first nine months of pregnancy.

This unity is prematurely and arbitrarily disrupted. The infant is thrust into a dangerous and destructive world, helpless. From the moment of his arrival, he begins a clinging, clutching, sucking, grasping, nuzzling set of maneuvers to reestablish the attachment necessary for his survival. These "attachment" behaviors automatically elicit in the normal mother a similar series of automatic responses: stroking, cuddling, cooing, etc. As the child matures, it will add to its repertoire of attachment maneuvers eye-to-eye contact, smiling, whining, pleading, gesturing, and all subtle mechanisms of ingratiation, seduction, and coercion to reinstate its attachment to the mother.

That attachment, as we have seen, is necessary for the child's survival and his emergence as a human being with precisely those qualities we most revere as being human. Since the human being requires some eighteen to twenty months of fetalization, of which only nine months can be spent within the womb, an alternative supportive and nourishing mechanism is required. The caring attention of the mother is the substitute for her womb—the persona of the mother replaces her placenta.

The union with the mother must be maintained for an adequate period of time so that when eventually it ends, that separation can be used for growth rather than attrition; for the self-pride and self-respect that permits a person to be in his own image worthy and capable of mature love. The child will proceed, again and again through life, to form metaphoric and mature versions of this early fusion through its identifications, ultimately being reunited, according to the myth of Aristophanes, in that other "symbiosis" that is defined as adult loving.

But growth is painful, and on the road to maturity, separation is necessary. Separation anxiety is the price we pay for autonomy.

CHAPTER VI

Separation

Much of the early consideration of attachment suffered from a confusion between the dependent, clinging behavior of an insecure child and attachment. The term "attachment," as it is used here, does not have the implication of insecurity or anxiety but denotes, rather, a normal stage of development. In its manifestations, attachment may seem identical to dependent behavior; but it is distinguished by its purposes from the attention-seeking behavior of the insecure child. Attachment is in the service of maturation; dependency is a substitute for it.

Through attachment, the helpless infant has found his way. In distress he called for help—and a willing ally responded. Having partially reinstated the security of the womb via this attachment to the mother; having repaired his sense of impotence by the delegation of his omnipotence to the parental figure; and having been reassured, by her protective responses, that the powerful mother will now serve his survival needs—what motivation could possibly exist for its abandonment? What allows the child to interrupt this "ideal state" to pursue the exploration of the world and to establish his independence? In a remarkable way it will be seen that it is precisely the successful attachment which grants the child the security, the renewed sense of strength, to allow for separation.

In the same developmental sense that attachment behavior emerges, separation is most likely a part of biological maturation. There is, in other words, a drive toward independence, a biological limit to taking and passivity. Attachment with the parent provides the sense of security which allows the child to pursue its natural curiosity in the exploration of the environment. The absence of attachment and the reassuring quality of such a protective environment would leave a child aware only of its impotence, and so too frightened to explore. Paradoxically, then, attachment is a step toward separation.

The intellectual curiosity of the preschool child is so uniformly present as to seem inevitable. The poking, prodding, exploring, examining, twisting, turning behaviors of a two-year-old are enough to exhaust the physical energies of any mother, in the same way that the incessant "Whys?" of the three- to five-year-old are enough to exhaust her intellectual capacities. It is a glory and a wonder whose later recall often leads to despair in the parent of a seventeen-year-old, who cannot understand where all that delight in learning and knowledge has gone. It is indeed an interesting question, whether this phenomenon is a natural cessation of intellectual curiosity with age, or a reflection (or indictment) of the educational system whose primary purpose, one would think, would be the sustaining of that function in its charges. Such curiosity is, after all, universally present in the children delivered into its hands.

The study of separation and contact is beset with the traditional problems inherent in studying our own behavior, and normal behavior in particular. The major difficulty in the study of a normal, essentially sound mother-child relationship is that where it exists, all kinds of behavior *other* than attachment predominate. When the baby is helped to be comfortable; when he feels secure, in settings that are familiar; and when his mother is available and around enough to satisfy him, the infant's attention will be free to be attracted to the outer environment, to be directed toward his surroundings.

At this stage of the child's development, he is more likely

to want the mother's services than the mother, and if her aid is enlisted, it is because she can be instrumental in helping him fulfill his aspirations in other directions. Her absence would inhibit that very pursuit so necessary for growth: exploration and manipulation of his world. The mother is necessary for the child to feel secure enough to learn to leave her. Most of the child's involvement in this period seems to be with his environment.

Another difficulty in studying attachment behavior is the obvious fact that we are not likely to disrupt the bond merely in order to test its strength. Much research is carried out that ought not to be, but despite the fact that certain cynical critics of science have repeatedly and rhetorically stated: "What can be done will be done," much that could be instigated to provide fruitful knowledge in the field of child development is *not* done. It is not done precisely because of the awareness that when dealing with human beings, we have an enormous special responsibility to make sure that observation does not extend into intrusion.

Since the moral right to experiment with human behavior is limited, one of the principal ways to study the inability to form attachments (and the results that ensue) has been to exploit the natural situations in which mothers absented themselves, and then to study the child's reactions to strangers.

Initially, a rather logical error was made in some of these studies, when it was tacitly assumed that the amount of distress shown by the child upon separation from the mother was proportional to the strength of his bond to her. But eventually a different and better interpretation of this distress arose. The infant's reactions to separation, and strangers, was seen as mediated by the *quality* of the relationship that existed between the mother and child. This served to place the question of security and insecurity into a central position. By this focus, then, an infant whose tie with his mother was strong and secure was seen as being *better* able to withstand short separations and better able to tolerate unfamiliar situations without too much distress; whereas an infant whose mothering experiences were inconsistent, insecure, or even rejecting would be much more at the mercy of the alien. Where the mothering was extremely poor, the child was likely to experience distressing panic upon even the temporary loss of the mother.

On the other hand, just as one must avoid the temptation to equate intensity of distress on separations with strength of attachment, one must avoid the counter-tendency to treat the behavior that results from separation—all the manifestations of separation anxiety—as either pathological or indicative of something wrong between mother and child. The need for the proximity of an attachment figure, and its increased urgency during periods of great stress, is a natural, widespread tendency to be found in the repertoire of many species; it is, after all, rational and intelligent to want one's protector close at hand. Far from being phobic or infantile, this tendency for the infant to view situations with alarm where he finds himself alone is perfectly justifiable and eminently sensible. To react with fear to common situations which seem frightening, such as a loud noise or sudden movement, is a natural part of any organism's signal system in the face of danger.

In this framework, it can be seen why separation anxiety must not be taken as an index of pathology, any more than it should be taken as an index of attachment. A more likely pathological sign is the total *absence* of anxiety upon separation from the mother. This is a clue that normal attachment, which must be seen as fundamental to independence, has not taken place—though, of course, when anxiety can be aroused with unusual readiness and intensity, this too is a sign of pathology.

It is beginning to sound here as though the mother, poor maligned creature, will turn out to be the one and only source of adult grief. But this is one of the dangers of focusing on a single crucial aspect of development without discussing others. Separation anxiety is a complex phenomenon and, like most aspects of human behavior, is multi-determined. Obviously there are many factors apart from the quality of mothering which affect a child's reactions to separation—the age of the child, his temperament, the cognitive development, the level of emotional maturity and ego development, the history of previous separations from the mother, the general nature of the child's defensive structure, as well as the child's history of exposure to strangers.

Numerous studies have shown that by utilizing a number of variable factors, much can be done to allay excessive anxiety at separation from the mother. Some are obvious: the presence of familiar surroundings and familiar faces, brothers and sisters or relatives or even familiar objects, such as dogs, toys, blankets—part of the folk wisdom of most families— have been experimentally demonstrated as reassuring; accessibility to photographs of the mother during prolonged separations can be helpful; all sorts of distractions, interesting sights, appeals to the child's intellect, even merely presenting the child with highly intriguing toys can be effective anxiety reducers, at least in short-term experimentally created separations.

It cannot be repeated too often that separation anxiety must be viewed as a typical reaction of the infant, indeed part of its heritage as a member of the species. It arises out of an original survival value and serves ultimately to create the secure environment which encourages the development of a strong and independent creature. What all studies seem to suggest is that separations early in life must not be taken with quite the casualness that they have been in the past, and that if such separations must take place, they should be kept as brief as possible.

A certain purism may have entered into the thinking of some early students, Bowlby in particular. Discoverers and innovators tend, in time, to overgeneralize early insights.

Bowlby was reinforced in his beliefs by the many studies of separation from the mother done on monkeys. He compares the effects of separation to the effects of smoking or radiation. In a study of rhesus monkeys, he says: "Although the effects of small doses appear negligible, they are cumulative. The safest dose is a zero dose." He seems to extrapolate the same conclusions to people. What he apparently neglects is a consideration of the autonomous rights of the mother, and the kind of frazzle that can be produced when a mother who no longer needs attachments (certainly not to an infant) for *her* security, feels bound by the imperative of "health" to be a twenty-four-hour-a-day, seven-day-a-week attendant to her child. There is a danger the child may then be seen as a jailer, hardly a conducive attitude for loving relationships.

It is probably true that there is a cumulative effect of separation. In typical test and retest situations, infants tended generally to be more anxious at the second occasion of separation than they were at the first; they were more clinging, staying closer to the mother when she was with them, and cried more when she was absent.

Particularly dramatic results were reported by C. Heinicke and I. Westheimer in their detailed study of 1966. One observer had been regularly present in the nursery where sixteen children resided during their separation from their parents. The children were from two to four years of age, and the length of their stay away from their parents ranged from twelve to seventeen days. The intensity of the children's response to the separation during the actual period of this stay at the nursery was great. All of them manifested the evidences of their outrage and despair, and only a couple of them gave signs of that detached ennui which signifies failure in attachment. The children cried incessantly; either clung desperately to a temporary mother substitute or angrily refused comfort from her; showed a loss of appetite, and a loss of bowel control. Typically regressive behavior of all sorts was reported in every child.

These findings were not unexpected; they merely confirmed the findings of various other studies. What was surprising and distressing was the long-term effect of this separation. One manifestation of this was evidenced in the following situation which was part of the experiment. Sixteen weeks later (a long time in the life of a child), after the return of the children to their parents, the observer who had been regularly present in the nursery came to pay a visit to the families of the children. Despite the presence of the mother in the room, the reassurance of the family surroundings, and sixteen weeks of elapsed time, all but one of the sixteen children recoiled at the sight of the observer and did their best to avoid him throughout the rest of the afternoon. The fact that this was a reaction to the lingering painful memory of the separation, and not merely that over the sixteen weeks the observer had become a stranger to the children, was testified to by the mothers' reactions. The mothers themselves were surprised that the child reacted in this way and found it totally atypical. They all confirmed that other strangers had visited and elicited no such responses as the child had visibly expressed in this reunion with someone associated with the testing experiment.

Other manifestations of the lingering effect of the separation were apparent. There was, as could be expected, a heightened sensitivity to *all* separations from the mother, even of the shortest duration. The children were for quite a time more clinging and "dependent," sleeping patterns were disrupted, and their sleep was generally disturbed and interrupted by crying at night.

Experimental studies on animals had anticipated the fact that a strong early attachment was one of the essential conditions for the development of an autonomous and independent adult. Harlow's infant monkeys raised with the terrycloth surrogate mother were (in its presence) a lot more adventurous than were the infants raised on the wire mesh surrogate mothers. Yet, as might be expected, the bravest and most curious infants were those who had been raised by their own mothers. It is obvious that despite all the warmth and softness that might be built into any inanimate mother, a machine is not a monkey, terrycloth is not skin, and no automaton can possibly compare in responsiveness and flexibility, in the multitude of responses, analyzable and non-analyzable, of the animate, natural mother. When we tease out for analysis a few factors in the overall quality of mothers, we are discussing only that fraction of them which current knowledge allows us to identify. These are always a pathetically small component of the variability involved in human loving and caring, which in their subtlety and complexity will always defy complete analysis.

The importance of the maternal presence is enormous and mysterious. The behavior of one-year-olds changes dramatically when the mother leaves an unfamiliar room, even though it is filled with all sorts of intriguing toys and diversions. Play and exploratory behavior either come to a dead stop, or continue at a significantly lower level of activity and complexity. Despite the fact that the toys are obviously just as interesting and plentiful, the children find them less and less appealing, and their anxiety is infinitely greater, in the mother's absence. On the other hand, as long as the mother remains in the room with the child, the child seems to ignore her presence. Despite a relative unfamiliarity with the setting, most of the children spend their time actively exploring, only occasionally turning around or looking to make a visual check on the mother.

Similarly, the manipulative play of two-year-olds will decrease by about 25 per cent when left alone with a stranger and by 50 per cent when left totally alone. At the same time, crying rises from a mere 5 per cent when the mother is present, to 30 per cent when she leaves the child with strangers present, and 50 per cent when he is left totally alone.

Obviously, what is referred to here as "separation" is not

specifically and exclusively the physical act, any more than the concept of attachment alludes merely to the physical proximity. What we are dealing with is a complex in which the physical action is a necessary condition for the establishment of an intra-psychic mechanism. If one is behavioristically oriented, and does not accept the concept of internalized images and intra-psychic mechanisms, it would be logical to expect that a child could be led to independence by merely conditioning him; we could simply introduce him to periods of increasingly frequent and increasingly long separation. That might indeed permit the toleration of separation, but separateness is not the point here. The separation is part of a chain of events, complicated and seemingly contradictory, which are intended to lead to independence and confidence. The intra-psychic event of separation is what is felt to be the necessary step in development.

The child must emerge from the symbiotic union with the mother if he is to learn to rely on his own resources. Somewhere along the line he must begin to define "her" as separate from himself. In order for the child to give up such a treasured love object, such an ensured source of safety, he must first have the security that he will not be abandoned by her. Attachment supplies such guarantees. It is the strength of that early attachment which builds the self-confidence that will allow for the establishment of the autonomous adult. Rollo May quotes Heidegger as stating that care is the basic constructive phenomenon of human existence: "When fully conceived, the care structure includes the phenomenon of selfhood."

Care alleviates anxiety, and anxiety is the enemy of all creativity and productivity. Every human being who has experienced fear—which means every human being—has learned the lesson. Anxiety, or fear, drives out desire; it impinges on attention; it destroys pleasure. It is disorienting and humiliating. Naturally, then, it will have a profoundly inhibitory effect on the life of a small child, particularly when we recognize just how tenuous and primitive is his security system. He has just begun to organize his activities. The automatic behavior that will come in later years is only now being established, and each new activity is an adventure in both delight and trepidation. But all of these ventures are necessary for that development of self-confidence and self-pride that is essential to maturity.

A sense of self and a trust of the self require what Erik Erikson has called a sense of mastery and what the psychologist R. W. White has called a feeling of efficacy. White described this feeling and its emergence in the following way: "Competence, in other words, is the cumulative result of the whole history of one's transactions with the environment. . . . Sense of competence describes the subjective side of one's actual competence. . . ."

I prefer the simpler term "self-confidence." At any rate, whatever the term—"mastery," "self-confidence," "sense of one's competence"—it obviously comes largely from the successful experiences of interacting with the environment. It is built on our experiences of ourselves as a doer we can trust and rely upon; on the sense of ourselves as, if not total "master of our fate," at least reasonable executor.

Play has been described as the activity where a child experiences the pleasure of "being the cause" in his interaction, but we have seen that play activity is severely limited when the child is insecure. If for no other reason, the disruption of this activity would explain why forced physical separation on a conditioning model is not conducive to the acquisition of self-confidence. Thus, instead of aiding and abetting the psychological weaning of the child from the mother, as a simple conditioning model would suggest, separation only enhances the negative effects invariably involved in the process and may lead to a self-deprecating individual who will always be dependent.

Forced separation will, further, inhibit the kind of more mature relationships which give meaning to adult life. The fact that a smooth, secure attachment with the mother enhances the ability to form adult attachments can be seen at a very early age in the direct correlation between attachment to the mother and the capacity to engage in interpersonal relationships with other figures. If, Mary Ainsworth writes, the child "attached himself to the mother he seemed to be able to form attachments to other caretakers, also, given the opportunity. If he did not attach himself to the mother he attached himself to no one."

Psychoanalysis does not have the advantage of the experimental and statistical methodology available to the developmental psychologist, and its case-reporting method will seem to some anecdotal, personal, and nonconclusive. To others, it compensates for the lack of numerical support for its conclusions by the conviction of the in-depth elaboration of the individual case. At any rate, by this point the data reported over so many years, even from conflicting schools of analytic thought, constitutes a statistical basis to establish the importance of an accessible, reliable, and good—or at least good enough—mother for the proper development of personality. Psychoanalytic reports from as early as 1938 emphasize that a person's "confidence" in the existence of supportive figures in the human environment is derived from repeatedly gratifying experiences with the mother during childhood. These experiences are the foundation on which a strong ego is built, capable of maintaining integration and self-regulation during periods when no support is available.

For Erikson, the mother-child relationship is the arena in which the first major conflict is played out that is to determine whether the personality is one of basic trust or mistrust. The eventual balance of these two alternatives is, of course, crucial to the development of almost any definition of a healthy, autonomous person. Only if the trust exceeds the mistrust can the infant start on the road to successful maturation, a process leading to autonomy. The feeling of mastery begins there and then.

Much of the research from the psychoanalytic literature depends on descriptions of behavior and the equation of such behavior with certain mental states. In many ways, this is the weakness of psychoanalysis and the strength of the developmental model. The mental states of children can only be inferentially induced retrospectively from the adult, or extrapolated from the behavior. As the child grows older, however, the actual event often becomes secondary to its symbolic representations. We live by the world we perceive, which is a different world from that which may actually exist. It is, nonetheless, the world that we occupy. The psychoanalytic point of view and psychoanalytic methodology emerge as particularly valuable with the growth of cognition, perception, and capacity for symbol formation; with the expansion of the internal representation of life; and with its projection onto the external world.

There is a problem, however, in categorizing very early separation anxiety as "signal anxiety." Signal anxiety implicitly assumes the capacity to anticipate and visualize the potential danger. It is not clear when the infant is capable of such conceptualization. It may be that early separation anxiety is an automatic anxiety, much more instinctually determined and less conceptually visualized. On the other hand, one might answer that since we judge this earliest separation anxiety by the behavior, it may be we, the observers, who are reading "anxiety" into it and that anxiety as an emotion only comes into existence when the signal is recognizable as dangerous—that is, when conceptualization occurs.

René Spitz, the child psychologist whose work in this area was seminal, also placed great emphasis on a stable mental representation of the mother. Spitz placed the fear of object loss at around eight months and on that basis takes the fear of strangers, which the infant experiences then, as an indication that the infant has already at that time some stable, inner representation of the mother.

Both developmentalists and psychoanalysts agree that separation requires a psychic sense of "mother." There is a major difference between psychoanalysts and students of Piaget, however, as to how complete the internalized symbol of the mother has to be for an internal representation to exist as a symbolic sense of the thing. Even within psychoanalysis, there is a spectrum of belief as to whether what is meant is a fully established internal representation of the mother, or merely a rudimentary scheme which permits the child to recognize his mother when she appears to him, and also distinguishes anxiety-producing discrepancies in that scheme when confronted by strangers. Spitz is generous in his readiness to see recognition even in the preferential smile the child reserves for the mother.

But surely the capacity for a mental representation, or abstraction of the meaning of "mother," is a determinant in the intensity of separation anxiety that will occur. After all, the child who has a true concept of what the mother is will be most keenly aware of what he may be about to lose in a separation. This can clearly be seen by comparing the difference in the reactions of children at various ages. When a group of infants admitted to a hospital was studied, a comparison was made between those below seven months and those above seven months. The older infants, as expected, showed greater stress at separation, reacted more negatively to strangers, clung more intensively at reunion with parents, and protested most strongly at any sign of impending separation. And in another study compared by age, it was apparent that the separation distress of the two-year-olds was much greater than that of the one-year-olds. In the study previously referred to, where photographs were shown to alleviate some of the separation anxiety, significantly it was the older children who benefited most from this technique. This would seem to confirm again that the internal representation was stronger, and that there was a direct relationship between the presence of a mental image and the capacity for anxiety and consequently reassurance by recalling the protective image.

The debate goes on as to when cognition has reached sufficient maturation so that the mother may be perceived as an autonomous and substantial figure and a stable representation of her can be simultaneously at the infant's disposal. For the mother's image to persist when she is absent, physically or psychologically, some maturation to a point of capacity to anticipate gratification and tolerate frustration is needed. By age two at least the typical, normal infant with strong attachment to a parent is able to use his internalized, stable representation of her to tolerate separation beyond the short term. In other words, to endure separation without anxiety more is needed than merely an inner representation of the mother: a level of ego strength, of self-confidence, must also be present.

It is interesting to note, however, that as the inner representation of the loved object continues to develop and becomes firmly established, cognitively as well as emotionally, anxiety about separation will decrease. If there is a distinction in the response to temporary separation and permanent loss, obviously the infant's intuitive understanding of this distinction is an absolutely crucial point. The child probably exhibits the most intense anxiety about separation in that period directly preceding his ability to make such distinctions. At that time, whenever the mother leaves, the infant has to contend with his fear of having lost her forever. When the child begins to discriminate between physical absence and true loss, he can begin to anticipate the diminution of separation anxiety. The child can endure separation as long as he can anticipate the future reappearance of the needed and loved figures.

He will, in time, find ways of keeping such figures at hand

even when they are not physically present at all. He will learn, via identification, to incorporate the parent—take her into and unto himself, for good and bad, for discomfort as well as comfort. For in that process of identification he will find both pain and pleasure, conscience and love. Separation is a crucial stage in the development of a mature and independent adult. Identification is an essential step in facilitating the development of a loving and caring adult.

CHAPTER VII

Identification

The development of the human body from that first fusion of sperm and egg to that most beautiful and wondrous of creatures, the young human adult, is such a profoundly complex mechanism that the awe and magic with which it is viewed by the amateur is only increased with professional knowledge. From those single-celled beginnings emerge intricate networks and interrelationships, biochemical systems, feedbacks, balances, and controls that make the most sophisticated of machinery seem always crude in analogy.

The functions of the human mind, the development of perceptions, emotions, cognition, memory, and imagination, parallel and transcend in wonder even the physical development. And always the interchange between the physical and the emotional, and the interchange between genetic directives and the nurturing environment, are the vital factors in facilitating normal development. The newborn human infant is so incredibly helpless that it would be crushed by the environment without the presence of protective parents; and even if there were some mechanisms to ensure physical survival, the dreadful sense of helplessness and vulnerability would certainly crush the spirit of a child. The early symbiosis that is represented in the attachment pleas of the infant and the parental responses gives the child more than just physical survival; it provides him with a sense of safety. He is helpless but not hopeless, and he sees his survival as guaranteed in the security of the loving relationship with the all-powerful parental figure.

From the secure base of attachment he is free to begin the separation which allows for his examination of the environment, even while still recognizing his inadequacy. The examination leads to pains and failures, but it is these which are the basis of an experience that will ultimately lead to success, and it is the successes that will be used to build a sense of confidence. He will learn that he is not quite so helpless as he had thought. Through the maneuvering and manipulating, exploring and poking, squeezing, tasting, stumbling, reaching, falling, discovering, despairing, conquering activities of the first few years, he will begin to build a sense of his own independence.

An independent creature is not, however, a loving or caring creature, nor necessarily a person prepared to receive love or support dependence. But independence is an essential step toward caring. One must first have the sense of adequacy, of personal resources, in order to lend or give some of one's supply to a helpless other.

In all probability the capacity for caring is part of the innate directive in our genes; the nurturing environment will simply allow it to emerge as do other late-developing characteristics, for example, secondary sexual characteristics. The "learning by experience," or coping type of behavior, is an expression of this directive. There is, however, an alternative mechanism whereby the human adult can massively shortcut traditional, experiential learning. One need not experience everything for one's self. There is the wholesale learning process termed "identification" whereby through an incorporation of another human being and his values, we are influenced in our behavior by that person and act as though we were directed by that other person with his entire sense of experience. Indeed, the whole cultural value system of generations of cumulative experience can be transmitted through the process of identification. Once we have incorporated an individual, we will reflexively respond in a way that will be approved by that internalized ideal.

We establish our sense of identity by a multiple set of maneuvers through varying ages. The first part of the process involves sensing one's self. When this begins it is hard to say. Many students of human behavior believe that probably there is some sense of one's self while still *in utero*. It is probably through the stretch motions of the proprioceptive system that we do have the experience of sensing the self. The next step, however, is to have a sense of one's self, that is, a sense of oneself, as differentiated from some other. The theories as to how precisely this emerges are multiple, and none of them are ever provable. Do we first experience the entire environment as projections of ourselves, from there begin to elaborate that which is alien and other, and, by definition, establish a sense of our own boundaries? Or is it best to visualize that early period as a matrix of mother-child from which the sense of one's self is hatched? However it happens, the division occurs, and from that time on we have a sense of the self as distinct from all that is not the self.

Then finally we must have a sense of self—not just body, not just entity, but the concept of our own personhood. It is this sense of self that is particularly facilitated through the processes of identification, and it is only one more irony of human development that we learn to love others only after first learning love of self.

Psychoanalytic theory is nowhere more confusing than in its implicit attitudes toward love. It placed sexuality at the center of life with a courage and brashness that shocked the Victorian world, and still shocks the spiritual descendants of that world; but it avoided romantic love like some shy adolescent. Yet basic to the psychoanalytic definition of a mature person is one who is capable of loving in all senses of the word.

If we look to the publications of Freud for discussion of

love, we will find only one series of papers devoted to that subject (*Contributions to the Psychology of Love*, 1910, 1912, 1918). When one eagerly turns to examine these papers, they prove to be essays on special problems of male impotence. One of the three papers describes the madonna / prostitute complex. It is as though psychoanalysis itself—in validation of its own theory about the Victorian era in which it was born—was able to accept its carnal occupation only when stripped from the tender, loving emotionality that should surround it.

Psychoanalysis has generally avoided the field of emotions. When, reluctantly and late, it came to deal with them, it found its primary interest in the darker emotions of rage and fear rather than the tenderness of caring. It will be seen that it was, in great part, through the gloomy necessity adequately to understand guilt and depression that psychoanalysis was precipitated into the awareness of identification which is at least a halfway point of love.

The neglect of emotion was almost inevitable, given the nineteenth-century model of medicine from which it emerged. It was facilitated, perhaps necessitated, by the libido theory and its enchantment with nineteenth-century energy concepts. Determined to establish a fixed instinctual nature in man (one major distinction of *Homo sapiens* being, ironically, the absence of such fixity), it studied the disposition of instinctual energy and neglected the emotional counterparts.

When the child was an isolated narcissist, in that primary state of magical omnipotence, all of his energy was seen as invested in himself. The child is not, by psychoanalytic theory, yet capable of love. He is that cloven creature of Aristophanes—that half-person, the individual who does not possess a loving partner. This, then, was called the autoerotic phase. To reach maturity it was essential for the developing human being to detach his libido from himself and his parts and find a way to invest (cathect) that libido on an external object. This capacity to cathect objects is what is meant by object relationships in the discussions that follow. "Object relationship" serves, among many of its meanings, to stand for the capacity to love. The peculiar and devious road to love requires first a symbiotic attachment in childhood. Then a period of separation, built on the strength of that attachment, gives the ego of the developing child an opportunity to grow and to exercise his capacity for "identification," another kind of fusion or joining far different from the attachment.

It was to the myth of Narcissus that psychoanalysis turned to symbolize this early period. Like Narcissus, fascinated and captivated by our own image, we occupy our early days exploring and loving only ourselves. But unlike the tragic youth of myth, we are not doomed to spend our days in this isolated pursuit, but are redeemed by an internal nature which liberates us from self-love and permits us to love others. Identification among other things is a particular form of first attachment to another person. By incorporating that person into ourselves, we are somewhere halfway between self-love and other-love, for that person with whom we identify is fused and confused into a new kind of matrix of self and other.

Identification was a concept that intruded constantly into Freud's thinking. He was primarily a clinician, desperately seeking alleviation of painful mental conditions. At the same time, he possessed the expansive mind of genius which led him to potential insights before he had the opportunity to integrate them into his broader theories. Freud dealt with identification independently in a number of different contexts where it was essential to the solution of other problems. He had little opportunity to explore the subject in its own right, and never developed a fully integrated and coherent hypothesis concerning it. For him, identification was primarily a tool with which to open other boxes; the process itself never commanded his full interest. Consequently, his views on identification were constantly modified to serve an appropriate purpose in relation to whatever work he was involved in at a given time, and this explains the inconsistency in his definition and use of the term. It remained for later writers to draw on the original works of Freud and on the richness and abundance of the developing fields of ethology, behavioral psychology, learning theory, and education to mold the current concept of identification.

Today, for the lay reader at least, this concept is most likely to be associated with the name of the brilliant psychoanalyst Erik Erikson, whose work on identification is unquestionably one of the major contributions to modern-day psychology. In a peculiar way, however, his work is less helpful for an understanding of loving and caring than one might have anticipated. Erikson also eschews tenderness, caring, and romantic love—although he does talk around them. He extended the concept of identification beyond Freud's psychosexual stages, but primarily in order to analyze the *social implications* of the developmental characteristics at each stage.

He focused essentially on the relationship between the individual and authority, not *an* authority or *the* authority in his life. He was interested in the relationship between the individual and his society as a whole. In a peculiar way, he therefore neglected the specifically interpersonal relationship between a particular man and woman, parent and child.

His deep concern with the dynamics of the broader picture required a selective attention to only certain aspects of human development; here again, one finds that he is much more interested in investigating those aspects of human behavior that deal with aggression and achieving mastery over the environment than with either caring or tenderness. Relationships are analyzed in terms of the power equilibrium, as defined by a specific culture. His work abounds in references to aggression, independence, leadership. It is in this area that he was the powerful pioneer, leading the way to understanding new dimensions in psychiatry. As to the tender emotions, he has been, I'm afraid, a true follower of Freud down the path of avoidance. An examination of the index of *Childhood and Society* is revealing. There are no entries for attachment, four entries for love, two entries for orality. There are, however, fifteen entries for anality and six for aggression. He chose to focus, for purposes of understanding identification, not on the oral and receptive activities but on anal-aggressive and muscular activities.

When emotion does appear, it is more likely to be shame and pride than love. It is in the competitive struggles that characterize the anal period, in toilet training (the battle of the pot) that Erikson starts the process of identification:

> Infantile sexuality and incest taboo, castration complex and superego all unite here to bring about that specifically human crisis during which the child must turn from an exclusive, pregenital attachment to his parents through the slow process of becoming a parent, a carrier, a carrier of tradition. Here the most fateful split and transformation in the emotional powerhouse occurs, a split between potential human glory and potential total destruction.

Glory and destruction are not ordinarily part of the everyday language of loving.

Even when Erikson deals with the oral stage, preceding the anal stage described above, his peculiar bias is apparent. The oral stage is that crucial phase in which basic trust or mistrust will be established and which will determine the quality and extent of the emerging autonomy. Yet even here Erikson prefers not to concentrate on the pleasures associated with feeding and the resultant loving bond that develops between mother and child; rather, the aspect of orality that Erikson chooses to emphasize is related to the control and mastery of aggression: biting, teething, grabbing, letting go. It is as though pleasurable orality is merely a frivolous prelude to the serious drama to emerge.

None of this is meant to fault Erikson or to diminish the

power of his contribution. It is simply to place his work in context, and to recognize why it did not, and inevitably could not, lead (although superficially it might have seemed as though it *ought* to have led) to an evaluation of love itself. It is person-to-environment, not person-to-person, that interests him. His approach, nonetheless, greatly expanded the horizons of psychoanalysis, which had been bound by its concern for person-to-self (i.e., intra-psychic) phenomena.

Whichever aspects are emphasized, identification remains a central mechanism used by an individual on his way to maturity; maturity can be measured in terms of a loving capacity, as well as mastery, control, or creativity.

Identification is related to concepts of modeling, the "wanting to be like" with which we are all familiar. We begin to choose as models those who seem more effective in satisfying our own needs than we are ourselves. A child identifies with his parents because they seem to possess the omnipotence that he feels necessary for his survival. As the child grows, at each stage of survival there will be other models with whom he can identify beyond the parents, individuals whose characteristics are more in accord with the wishes and needs of that particular stage.

All of this identification occurs at an unconscious level and not, as it may have sounded, with the full volition of the subject involved in the selection. Also, one ought not to think of identification as an all-or-none phenomenon. We are quite capable of selecting some qualities from an individual with whom we choose to identify and ignoring others. In most respects there is a differential selectivity in which only those features are incorporated that are felt to be of help in the achievement of one's necessary goals at the time. With the child, where all things are easier to see, one notices identification with animals, institutions, abstract ideas, and eventually fictional characters. Beyond all this, the central identification is with one's own fellow human beings, and the primary ones are the parents.

When we speak of one's identity, what we are talking about is the accumulation of the numerous identifications made throughout one's lifetime. As in most aspects of behavior, the whole is different from the sum of its parts. The infinite combinations integrated into identities make for the marvelous variety and individuality that characterize the human species. This identification allows for the mastery of environment; it is essential in the establishment of conscience; it is the mechanism through which each individual internalizes the good and the affect that he sees in others in his environment. It is through identification that each individual is allowed to perpetuate the achievements, attributes, values, and qualities that define humanness and personhood.

The identification also permits the capacity for love. Unfortunately, it does not guarantee the capacity. We can in a particularly bitter perversion identify with the aggressor; that is, if sufficiently abused, we can undertake a denial of loving in which we will learn cruelty by the cruelty that is visited on us.

But the beginning drives are always toward emulation of the caring figure—if only one is present. It is a delight to watch a little boy imitate the posture of his father or a little girl imitate the gestures of her mother. It is even more delightful to see the child, willy-nilly, without any conscious knowledge on his part, begin to shape his behavior into infantile patterns of his perception and vision of the parental behavior.

In the beginning, of course, love and identification are not differentiated. They both occur in relation to the same object, the mother. These were originally referred to as "primary identifications." The mother, at this point, is most likely seen by the infant as an extension of himself and not as a separate entity with an independent existence. This is precisely that symbiotic period discussed earlier. It is in this stage that "the hungry infant's longing for food, libidinal gratifications, and physical merging with the mother, which is the precursor of future object relationships, is also the origin of the first, primitive type of identification," according to the psychoanalyst Edith Jacobson.

This extremely early identification with the mother has an automaticity unparalleled in later identifications. Consistent with the general rudimentary quality of the self, it seems to be much more genetically fixed than the future process of identification. Here it is imitative and almost automatic; what the mother is and does, the child will be and will do. The mother's role at this point is to set the cornerstone, the very foundation, upon which all future identifications must stand. As such, she unconsciously exercises the greatest control over the future development of the child's personality. For it is she, almost alone, who is the foundation of the earliest, all-critical identifications.

This has been poetically described by another psychoanalyst, Lichtenstein, as the process by which the mother truly gives birth to the individual her infant will become. Through the care and devotion, through the energy and love, that she invests in the child, she guarantees "the infant's becoming the child of his particular mother."

Identification is a peculiar process. It operates on an unconscious level. While a mother may wish to design a child according to certain personal standards, she is more likely to influence the design of a child by mechanisms over which she has little conscious control. There is an interesting creative interplay between the two, with each assuming the appropriate role where the mother is often no more aware of the part she is playing than the child is of his. Her intellectual direction of the child will of course influence him to a certain extent; but it is primarily other mechanisms that mold and shape the personality of her child—sometimes in the direction to fulfill her expectations of him, sometimes unconsciously and ironically to create an individual who will serve motives she does not understand, for purposes which she will later consciously reject. In fascinating studies of psychopathic children who acted out antisocial behavior, it was demonstrated that the child was acting out specific behaviors unconsciously encouraged by the parent even while the parent was consciously appalled and distressed by the behavior.

The process, of course, is not completely dominated by parent or environment. Any mother of more than one child can testify to the fact that infants have potentials (personalities?) of their own, and while not unlimited, this rudimentary potential will constrict the mother and demand certain types of interactions. The infant will respond more readily to some behaviors than he will to others, and the mother who wants peace of mind will soon find a rapprochement with the child's genetic potentials. The process has been described by the brilliant child psychoanalyst Margaret Mahler as a "mutual selection of cues." Mutual, of course, here does not imply equality of control exerted over the selection of processes. This process has also been described as a mirroring, or echoing, effect. By this is meant that the mother reflects back to the infant his first sense of himself. The reflection occurs by touch, smell, receptivity, and other primitive sensations. What begins then slowly to emerge are the outlines of the child as reflected in the mother. Gradually an incipient sense of self, a sense of identity, begins to arise in the child in reaction to the constancy of some of these reflected patterns.

In addition to the mirroring, another process closer to learning theory and conditioning is involved. This has to do with the pragmatic trial-and-error method employed by the developing human child in establishing character traits. Psychoanalysis tends to see human behavior as being strung across a series of polarities of personality. One such polarity is the character spectrum which places oral (hysterical) traits at one end and anal (obsessive) at the other. We now acknowledge phallic, narcissistic, and paranoid personality elements too, but the original primary polarity will suffice here.

The hysterical personality is seen as someone emotionally immature, strongly suggestible, imaginative, emotionally labile, with urgent needs to be loved and admired, and a strong dependency on approval of others for self-esteem. The obsessive is work-oriented, perfectionistic, emotionally constricted, and with a strong conscience. Most people have oral and anal aspects fused in their personality. Traditionally, personality type has been seen as being determined by the nature of one's "fixations." This in itself may simply be a form of shorthand language for describing the adaptive pattern of development. What I suspect happens is that the child is prepared to try *all* means of satisfying the parent and gaining its approval. If it finds that being cute, charming, ingratiating, or cuddly evokes a response of approval or for-giveness for wrongdoing from the parent, it is likely to use those mechanisms more and more as means of handling confrontation and conflict. If the parent responds to such ingratiation and charm with distaste because she cannot tolerate it, the child may find alternate means of approval. The way to this mother's heart may be through "being a good boy" and doing all that that implies: tidying up his room, playing quietly by himself, attending to the "work" of his specific age period. This child will then see performance and achievement rather than charm and ingratiation as a primary means for gaining approval, and will tend more and more to use the proven means of pleasing the parent.

The hysteric learns the lesson that the *expression* of emo-tion is a means of security, while the obsessive learns that the *control* of emotion is a means of security. The difference is also in terms of which emotions predominate: the obsessive feels safe because of what he *does*, therefore he is threatened when his performance fails; the hysteric feels safe because of what he *is*, and he feels threatened when he feels unwanted or unloved. The hysteric seems implicitly to be saying, "You take care of me, because I am lovable and worthy of being taken care of." The "you" is brought into constant consciousness. The obsessive seems to be saying, "I will be taken care of if, or because, I am good (obedient, dutiful)." The figure by whom he is to be taken care of is repressed or abstracted.

The child, amoeba-like, will try anything in the early years of development to gain parental approval; as the amoeba recoils from the noxious and ingests the nutritive, so will the developing child learn that which is effective for his survival, which may explain the "hereditary" nature of personality—that little Italian children tend to behave like Italians, whereas Swedish children generally tend to behave like Swedes. It is interesting to speculate how much more tolerant most parents are of ingratiation and cuteness on the part of a girl than of a boy. It is not surprising, therefore, that more women are driven into hysterical behavior patterns and more men into obsessive. This is not to suggest that this is the only mechanism. But there is no question that much of what passes as gender behavior, as typically "masculine" or "feminine," is the elected design of the parents who force the child in the direction which gives them security. A father is likely to be threatened by overt affection, warmth, demonstrativeness on the part of a son since this is patently "unmanly." He will therefore help to contribute to that artificial gender stereotype of manliness which will reciprocally determine the model for each future generation. Approval-seeking, then, is one ad hoc means of modeling one's self to parental standards.

Earlier I described the distress created by the occasional unavailability of the mother. Now it is important to recognize the adaptive value of separation—if brief, limited, and at the appropriate time of development. It forces the child to begin to identify the point at which the mother's boundaries end and his own begin. Separation, like frustration, is a necessary part of the child's experience if it is to develop the increasingly sophisticated cognitive abilities we expect of the adult. We want the child to establish a realistic self-representation distinct from, and unfused with, the mother's.

It is only when the child begins to realize that he is not the mother that the period dominated by attachment can end and the period of identification take precedence. The knowledge that the infant is not the mother initiates the more realistic effort to become *like* the mother. The child may be said to realize that at this point, the best way of regaining the power enjoyed during the period of union with the mother is to begin being his own mother, that is, to begin doing for himself what previously the mother could do. This, then, is the start of the process that is to continue through adulthood and is perhaps the most important single vehicle for change and growth. And so we find, ironically, the roots of individuality in imitation.

Obviously it does not take long for the child to become aware that he is different from the parent; the awareness that he is different will be a major impetus for identification, a major part of the process of learning to do for oneself. Those particular aspects of the parent that the child chooses to identify with will in the process of identification become internalized and blended in with the remainder of that child's specific character traits. The purpose is not to become the other, but rather to assimilate those aspects of the other until they are coherent with the person's already existing and functioning self.

When love or admiration are expressed exclusively as a wish for *total* fusion, the individual may be in for real trouble. The desire to actually *be* the other person, or the actual belief that one *is* another, is seen to be founded in the loss of boundaries between self and the surrounding environment of objects. This loss of boundaries is, of course, a serious matter and is a symptom of one of the most severe personality disturbances, either in patients who regress to this state or those who never "hatch out" of the symbiotic fusion.

There is a tendency, however, for some authors to overstate the separateness; and while, of course, an individual must never think he is other than himself, one of the truest measures of real love is when there is a confusion of ego boundaries between self and loved one to the extent that one's own pleasures and pains seem indistinguishable from those of the other. Certainly one of the indices of love is when one experiences the pain of the loved object with as great acuity as one's own. And one of the truest tests of love is the sense that, while knowing there are differences between one's self and the person loved, we find ourselves, at least on an unconscious level, continuously confused as to where they begin and we end. Freud says that, ". . . at the height of being in love the boundary between the ego and the object threatens to melt away. . . . A man who is in love declares that 'I' and 'You' are one and is prepared to behave as if it were a fact." That such phenomena may be seen as both a sign of "craziness" and a sign of love lends a certain credence to the popular notion that people in love are a little bit crazy.

Originally the relationship between identification and protective, caring, tender character traits was not well understood. Psychoanalysis was born in psychotherapy; that is, its primary energies and concerns, particularly in the early days, were devoted to the treatment of the mentally ill. It therefore concentrated on anxiety, tension, withdrawal, depression, and the other agonies of emotional distress. With elaboration, it began to see the *absences* of phenomena as also representative of serious mental illness and was free to search for those quality traits that are essential for a person to be considered normal or healthy.

It was only with the birth of child psychiatry that we began to conceive of identification as an aspect of normal development and to recognize that, as the English psychoanalyst Joseph Sandler astutely pointed out, it was "by no means always a substitute for an object relationship, nor is it always used defensively." It was indeed then discovered that the child's capacity for love and identification, in the words of Edith Jacobson, "evolved hand in hand and exercised a mutually beneficial influence on [parent and child]."

When identification was still viewed as defensive in nature, it was seen either as an expression of an emotional tie binding the parent to the child and/or as a device used by the child to allay anxieties caused by his inability to be sure of the parent. All of this was viewed as emerging out of the competitive struggles inherent in the oedipal complex. In order to reduce the anxiety caused by an anticipated struggle, and therefore forestall possible abandonment by the parent of the same sex who is seen as the rival, the oedipal child "identifies" with his would-be rival. Afraid that he can't "lick 'im," he "joins" him.

For a long time this defensive concept of introjection and identification so dominated Freudian literature that authors had to suggest apologetically that identification could act in the services of love, and reintroduce the idea in this format. But identification, as we now see, can be for positive reasons, and eventually is the basis for much that dignifies human behavior. It is part of the uniqueness and glory of the human being that this process, born in love and for love, eventually also becomes the mechanism for creativity, work, and achievement that forms so significant a part of a uniquely human existence. It is the "Lieben und Arbeiten" that Freud saw as the purpose of life. There is no reason why the same mechanism cannot serve different purposes. For surely love and work can both be seen as cornerstones of self-confidence, self-pride, and self-esteem, those ultimate ingredients whose presence or absence determines pleasure or pain, fulfillment or frustration, health or neurosis.

Similarly, there is another polarity that ought to be put to rest. Some advocates insist that the concept of identification is purely a narcissistic and self-serving process, since its primary motive is to enhance self-esteem; while others insist that identification is a variation on the theme of object relationship, i.e., in the service of love. The latter would hold that the principal purpose of identification is desire to solidify the emotional tie, binding the individual to the object of his love. It is ridiculous to make these two mutually exclusive. Even cursory examination shows that self-esteem and self-love are essential first steps in the capacity for giving love to others. Only when we value ourselves are we able to value the feelings that others have for us, and only when we see ourselves as worthy enough can we allow ourselves the freedom to have feelings for others.

Having discussed briefly the purposes of identification and the results of identification, something remains to be said about the process itself. How do identifications occur; how do we select our models? One result of identification is to effect a change in us, making us more like the object with which we identify. This is an unconscious process, but that does not deny the possibility that there are conscious counterparts; it does not exclude the possibility of conscious attempts to emulate. However, even the conscious choices we make, as to which individuals or which features we will try to identify with, will be determined by unconscious factors of our earlier identification. These will either be in direct relationship to the parent we thought we had, to the parent we wished we had, or as a corrective antidote to the one we did have. The early encapsulated parent, of whom we may not be aware, inevitably will determine, directly or indirectly, even our conscious emulations. Some have attempted to make a distinction between imitation, which is seen as having no history of antecedents, and identification. To a psychoanalyst, however, the concept that there can be adult behavior which has no antecedents is remote.

It is often difficult, short of psychoanalysis, to determine when identification has taken place, since the two major criteria generally are a restructuring in the psychic organization of the individual, and a significant alteration in the individual's sense of himself. It is only when we sense over time that we are becoming other than we were that we can appreciate the force of identification with whatever model we have chosen.

In the process of identification, the subject then becomes more like his *idea* of the model, not necessarily like the model in actuality. Identification is not a category of *behavior*, nor do its most important manifestations necessarily directly affect behavior. A human being is not merely the sum total of his behaviors, important as they may be. Identification essentially acts upon the underlying organization of the personality, such as attitudes, values, self-representation, and motivations. These in turn will of course effect behavioral changes which can then be observed; through such observation of behavior, we may retroactively begin to reconstruct the organization that underlies it. Either way, it is the internalized mechanism that is the crucial factor.

Beyond all else, "identification is one of the main mechanisms by which a child becomes the organizer and initiator of independent, adaptive activities," according to child psychiatrists Ritvo and Solnit. Whenever a person's sense of control over his own life is expanded; whenever he is seen as more and more the source of his own pleasures and security, his pride increases, his self-esteem increases, and his capacity for loving is enhanced with them. Increased autonomy does not make one less desirous or needful of others. The opportunity to sense one's self as a competent person, as an independent person, and as a coping person allows one the generosity, unavailable to the neurotic and the narcissist, of sharing oneself with others and of exposing oneself to the vulnerability that loving inevitably implies. When an individual can be more independent and self-reliant, fewer of his relationships have to be centered around the rather unreciprocal fulfillment of his own personal needs.

He can then proceed on to greater mutuality. This capacity for forming truly mutual relationships is one of the key characteristics of healthy love.

One of the enormous advantages of the developing concept of identification is that it introduces a ray of hope that seemed foreclosed by early psychoanalytic theory, which tended to see personality as essentially fixed by age three or four. This is not to deny that Freud was correct in sensing the enormous leverage of these early years. A sufficiently severe deficit in the first year of life will never be rectifiable. It does mean that with the typical child who falls somewhere between the extreme of perfect health and total deprivation, certain failures in the models presented can be modified by surrogates and substitutes. Identifications are not static. They are in a state of dynamic flux, and one builds one's ego step by step. One can extend, elaborate, and revise, or combine a basic identification with other identifications. In this sense identification is best seen as a process, rather than a distinct structure or entity. While it is unlikely that early identifications ever completely disappear, to say that something is ineradicable does not mean that it cannot be modified.

Of course, with increased growth and maturation the sense of self must become fixed to permit that automaticity of behavior which alone facilitates an unself-conscious life. The rules cannot be constantly changing. Our perceptions cannot change from day to day; such confusion would destroy any sense of integrity and security. Therefore, as development advances and the individual grows older, each new identification has an increasingly smaller effect. This is another reason why those initial identifications with the parent have such a tremendous impact in the creation of the personality of the child. They are the first. They are seeded in virgin soil. And the impact of each further identification can only be felt via its influence on the primary identification.

The models and images that the specific parents present to the child in early life will influence the person he is to become as much as the genes they have already supplied. Our genetic inheritance is expanded by cultural transmissions. With the magic ingredient that only *Homo sapiens* possesses, we are capable of selecting beyond the accident of our parental environment and building at least part of ourselves in our own selected images. All those figures whom we love and admire, we carry with us. They become the mortar and cement of the stable person: they serve our conscience, our capacity to love, and our potential for aspiration and achievement.

The mechanism of identification can also account for the fact that cultural, cognitive, interpersonal, and emotional features are often shared with an amazing consistency by every member belonging to a culture, and passed on to every new member of the culture who must, in order to develop in every way, start out by identifying with some older member of this cultural group. In our pursuit of individualism, therefore, we must never forget the fact that there is no such thing as an individual human being outside the nexus of his social environment. As G. H. Mead puts it:

> . . . Human nature is something social through and through, and always presupposes the truly social individual. Indeed, any psychological or philosophical treatment of human nature involves the assumption that the individual belongs to an organized social community, and derives his human nature from the social interactions and relationships with that community as a whole and with the other individual members of it.

We are not and never can be "individual." The paradoxical lesson of identification is that we achieve our unique selves via our fusion with others. Whatever individualism means, it is something we can only gain through early attachments to, later identifications with, and, finally, loving of other people. To find ourselves we must embrace others. It is a peculiar creature that is so constructed.

Only in human creatures is the self not merely defined and distinguished *from* the other, but defined in terms of at least some others. Further, that which is most singularly human about our behavior, that which elevates us above the animal host, arises from love of others and depends on care from others. Not only is our genetic pattern reticulate as Huxley has described it; in a sense, humanness is a reticulate phenomenon, a network whose real meaning is only appreciated by the extensions that bind each knot of individuality to the next, creating the social fabric in which personhood has true existence. The individual is an illusion. If we unravel the network of social contacts, the knots disappear.

CHAPTER VIII

Conscience

Animals are so constructed that they tend to be aware—to the degree they possess self-awareness—of that part of their behavior which serves individual purposes; in the same way, they tend to be ignorant of the automatic behavior built into them that serves species purposes. As a result, when that most aware of animals, the human being, behaves selfishly, it seems natural to his own purposes and true to himself. Aggression, competitiveness, avarice, selfishness, are often seen as "lack of control," as "giving in to our nature"; whereas unselfishness, generosity, and self-sacrifice are visualized as learned or imposed phenomena. Even when we do construct a concept, such as conscience, which sees unselfish behavior as directed by internal mechanisms, it is conceived of as part of the learning of civilization. And even when goodness is recognized as internalized, it is viewed as an internal artifact—an homuncular foreign body abrasively occupying our inner spaces, an irritant for good.

If one's frame of reference focuses on the individual, caring seems self-sacrificing. But if the focus is on the group, on the species, it is the ultimate self-serving device—the sine qua non of survival. Generosity and unselfishness, particularly in the face of the weak and helpless young, are the essential ingredients of species survival. Identification is a means by which we incorporate the values of our group into the motivational system that directs our behavior. Conscience is that and more.

One of the great students of conscience in American life was that nineteenth-century social commentator, Mark Twain. In a particularly illuminating episode, he dramatizes our ambiguities in the face of our better selves. It is a scene that traditionally evokes a sense of delight over the sweet rightness of things, a scene that has been played out weekly in movies and hourly on television. The forces of evil are conquered, the bad are subdued, the good triumph, and virtuous order is restored. Yet Huckleberry Finn, that Everyman (Everyboy?) of nineteenth-century America, is distressed. The Duke and the Dauphin, the two scoundrels who have used and abused him, exploited, ridiculed, humiliated, and mocked him, are receiving their comeuppance. But as Huck watches these two conmen being tarred, feathered, and railroaded out of town, his emotions surprise him:

> . . . I see they had the king and the duke astraddle of a rail—that is, I knowed it *was* the king and the duke, though they was all over tar and feathers, and didn't look like nothing in the world that was human—just looked like a couple of monstrous big soldier-plumes. Well, it made me sick to see it; and I was sorry for them poor pitiful rascals, it seemed like I couldn't ever feel any hardness against them any more in the world. It was a dreadful thing to see. Human beings *can* be awful cruel to one another.

> . . . So we poked along back home, and I warn't feeling so brash as I was before, but kind of ornery, and humble, and to blame, somehow—though *I* hadn't done nothing. But that's always the way; it don't make no difference whether you do right or wrong, a person's conscience ain't got no sense, and just goes for him *anyway*. If I had a yaller dog that didn't know no more than a person's conscience does I would pison him. It takes up more room than all the rest of a person's insides, and yet ain't no good, nohow. Tom Sawyer he says the same.

The words that Twain uses in an attempt to dissect the emotions of conscience are enormously sophisticated and not redundant. They are the words that only a student of conscience, or an intuitive genius, would have used: "ornery," "humble," and "to blame."

"Ornery" has an implication of anger, resentment, and meanness, and suggests both Huck's identification with the victims and his identification with the lynch mob. Angry at the victims, he is nonetheless angry with the mob that treats them so cruelly. Ultimately he is angry with himself for identifying with that mob and, probably, for having wished the same many times over on these two men. He is experiencing a truth that has been recognized by many, that the literal fulfillment of our fantasies rarely offers pleasure. Fantasies are meant to be fantasies only, gratifying within the safe bounds of the knowledge that they exist not in this real world.

He feels humbled, lowered, reduced, humiliated, because he is viewing the darker and baser side of human behavior. With a social conscience that he possesses unawares, he recognizes that what he sees in others, he shares with them as a member of the human race. If people have this capacity for meanness, then, as a person, he is viewing that lesser part of himself.

And, finally, he feels to blame somehow—he, who has every right to demand vengeance, to enjoy retaliation, and has done nothing to harm these men. Somehow or other, he shares a common burden of guilt with those who violate decency by treating fellow human beings with such indignity.

"Feeling to blame" is as good a definition of guilt as we are likely to have. Guilt is one of the most readily misunderstood of the commonly experienced emotions. To define "guilt" as an emotion is in itself considered a misuse of the word by that most elegant standard, the Oxford English Dictionary, which lists a number of definitions of "guilt," none of which includes the emotional state. Quite the contrary, it gently cautions us against its "misuse for 'sense of guilt,'" citing for reproach a Reverend Tillotson who called guilt: "nothing else but trouble arising in our mind from a consciousness of having done contrary to what we are verily perswaded was our Duty."

I am afraid I must join the Reverend in reproach. "Guilt" as it will be used here will refer not to a "delinquency," "fault," "responsibility," or the "fact or state of having committed a wrong," but indeed to the "sense of guilt." In other words, "guilt" will be defined as an emotion, the "remorseful awareness of having done something wrong" (American Heritage Dictionary of the English Language).

Perhaps part of the problem with dictionary definitions of emotions is that by their very nature, emotions defy definition. In that sense they are immune to the kind of analysis to which behavior is typically exposed. Emotions are difficult to quantify, difficult to communicate between people, difficult even to distinguish qualitatively one from the other. The behaviorists, by avoiding emotions and dealing only with their behavioral manifestations, are allowed a kind of precision that dynamic psychologists can never have. But something is lost. Emotions can at times be identified (and at times not even that) by their accompanying behavior, but not necessarily explained, or even understood, in those terms. In normal communication one person describes his emotion to another by resorting to a type of question that starts with: "You know how you feel when . . . ?"

The peculiar fact is that many people do *not* know "how they feel when." Many people confuse and misunderstand the nature of the emotions they may be experiencing. The degree of misunderstanding of one's own emotional state varies with the emotion. For example, most people will recognize fear. On the other hand, to an observer (a psychoanalyst), people will often seem visibly and obviously angry and yet have no genuine awareness that they *are* angry; or worse, they misinterpret their anger as another emotion. It is not uncommon to hear a clearly angry patient talk about feeling agitated or anxious.

Feelings of depression are, I suspect, more often than not misread. Customarily, individuals who are depressed will not even be aware of being in the grip of an emotional state. They are more likely to complain of exhaustion, fatigue, boredom, weariness, etc. When a patient states that he is chronically tired and then describes the fact that he has had precipitous weight loss and insomnia, that is—barring physical illness—a better description of depression than when a patient says, "I am depressed."

Guilt is more often than not confused with something that is better defined as "guilty fear." When people are asked to describe a situation in which they recently felt guilty, they most often describe the hand-in-the-cookie-jar syndrome, for example, speeding down the highway, aware of the siren, and the "sense of guilt." In most of those situations the central emotion is not guilt but fear. Here guilt is merely an adjective modifying the fear. It is the fear that one is about to receive punishment; it is guilty fear because of the sense that the punishment is deserved. The emotion, however, is still fear. It is the awareness that we are about to have something unpleasant inflicted on us which, however, we deserve.

If we are experiencing guilty fear, there is an enormous sense of elation and relief when the footsteps at the door at the moment our hand is in the cookie jar turn out to be those of a younger brother; or when the whizzing siren goes past us and apprehends the "perpetrator" in the car ahead of us. The relationship of true guilt to punishment, however, is entirely different, and that may be one of the true distinguishing signs between the two. True guilt does not stand or fall on impending punishment. Indeed, true guilt is usually at its worst when there is no punishment entailed; it is relieved at the possibility of punishment. True guilt, to return to Mark Twain, is experienced when Jim describes slapping his daughter for disobedience, unaware that she is deaf. If true guilt is in relationship to any authority, it is to that authority we vest within ourselves, which by its fusion ceases to have the quality of "other" that a conflict with authority implies. True guilt *seeks*, indeed embraces, punishment; it is alleviated or mitigated by such acts. The relief that confession and, even more so, expiation in penance bring to the guilty must have been experienced by every reader. Martin Buber in his criticism of psychoanalytic interpretations of guilt, in *The Knowledge of Man*, recognized just such confusion about the nature of guilt in Freud:

> . . . Guilt was simply not allowed to acquire an ontic character [by Freud]; it had to be derived from the transgression against ancient and modern taboos, against parental and social tribunals. The feeling of guilt was now to be understood as essentially only the consequence of dread of punishment and censure by this tribunal, as the consequence of the child's fear of "loss of love" or, at times when it was a question of imaginary guilt, as a "need for punishment" of a libidinal nature, as "moral masochism" which is complemented by the sadism of the superego. "The first renunciation of instinctual gratification," Freud stated in 1924, "is enforced by external powers, and it is this which creates morality which expresses itself in conscience and exacts a further renunciation of instinct."

Buber is correct—and yet, not correct, for as in most cases the richness of Freud's mind encompassed over the years most possibilities. And his stubbornness (obsessiveness?) would not allow him totally to abandon any of his conceptual models. A closer examination of the evolution of the concept of conscience reveals the twists and turns in Freud's thinking with each accretion of new knowledge, and in many ways maps out our current thinking about the sources of conscience.

The origins of Freud's thinking on conscience mechanisms

can be traced all the way back to the *Studies in Hysteria* of 1893. Breuer and Freud had elaborated a concept of the etiology of hysteria—then visualized as a neurological disease —based on the "encapsulation" of ideas during hypnoid states. This in itself was a revolutionary contribution to medicine. It established the principle that an individual could suffer what seemed like physical disease because of ideas or "reminiscences."

Freud conceived of a mechanism for hysteria based on the psychic concept of defense. It was an inspired difference. In this concept, if an idea was unbearable to the individual, it was *relegated* to the unconscious as a means of protecting himself from awareness, rather than slipping into the unconscious as through a door carelessly left open. This concept—repression—is fundamental to psychoanalytic theory. By Freud's conceptualization of the defense neurosis, the individual was moved from the position of a victim of his neurosis to the role of a participant in it. In that step, psychiatry was changed from a static to a dynamic frame of reference. From then on, attention would be paid to the forces *and counterforces* whose resultants determine the course of human behavior.

Freud had no difficulty in elaborating a theory of such forces, and quickly mobilized them under the category of the instinctual drives for pleasure. The ultimate expression of this was, at least in the early days, the libido. But what were the counterforces that kept a person from selfishly and ruthlessly pursuing his instinctive pleasures? What was the source of the unselfish, the generous, the self-denying, the caring? Whence did they arrive? What was their nature? Their source of energy? Their dynamic past? These problems plagued Freud throughout his intellectual life, and he would vary his interpretation of the repressive forces depending on the context in which he was analyzing the drives. There was no problem in understanding that people seek pleasure and satisfaction. What precisely keeps them from the complete gratification of their drives was more difficult to conceptualize; and that, of course, is the stuff of conscience.

In the 1890's, Freud was to refer to concepts of shame, disgust, revulsion, and loathing as forces of repression. He accepted, unanalyzed, the presence of these limiting social and moral forces. But when a full-scale analysis of instinctual drive was formulated in 1905, it demanded some explanation for repressive forces beyond that which had previously been offered. In his explanation of the cessation of sexual activity which occurs in the years just prior to puberty, Freud saw the overwhelming power of the incest taboo as the essential repressive influence. Here, then, for the first time was the suggestion of an innate, genetically determined mechanism for *inhibiting* certain behavior, a mechanism which will be brought into play independent of the life experience of the individual.

In this period Freud increasingly begins to use the general term "counter-cathexis" for these inhibitory forces, and while it is descriptive, it evades the central issue. Shortly after this, Freud evolved the concepts of reaction formation and sublimation as defenses. "Reaction formation" was defined as a defensive maneuver, which neutralized and denied certain unacceptable impulses, thoughts, or ideas by relegating them to unconsciousness and by embracing the opposite. "Sublimation" is the mechanism by means of which the energy that would have been used for repressed impulses (traditionally, sexual impulses) is utilized for "higher social and cultural aims." A desire for fecal smearing might, for example, be handled by sublimation via an interest in the molding of clay, or by a reaction formation in which the child becomes excessively tidy and orderly and absorbed with cleanliness. Here Freud specifically classified such emotions as loathing, disgust, guilt, shame, and morality as examples of reaction formation. In time, he began to allude to "an unconscious sense of guilt" (1907), and finally brought this to full expression in his examination of the anal character (1908).

The first full treatment of an organized conscience as a primary phenomenon, not as defensive reaction to an impulse, occurred in the previously described paper, *Totem and Taboo* (1912). Again, I would like to emphasize that the importance of this paper does not rest on the concept of the primal horde, nor necessarily on what it has to say about primitive religions, the nature of totems or of specific social taboos. For our purposes, the most crucial aspect of this work is that Freud now conceived of a relatively autonomous and independent set of behavior-controlling and impulse-limiting mechanisms—taboos, if you will—that are part of the genetic endowment handed down from parent to child. These limitations on the selfish pursuit of the instincts are a genetically determined part of the species characteristic that enforces those civilized behavior patterns which facilitate social living. Social living, then, is now not a part of learning nor an accident of a culture which managed to control in time the destructive and individualistic impulses of its constituent members. The group itself is a genetic fact of man's nature, and the assurances for group survival are part of the protoplasmic component of each individual member of the group.

When you strip *Totem and Taboo* of the specifics of its content, the relevance of the total theory seems most impressive as an image of man in a network of supporting relationships. It pictures that network as the true boundary of personhood. The social unit not only limits, but defines, the nature of human beings. This, then, was Freud's statement on conscience in his earliest period of development. Throughout this period there is one common thread which binds the theories of conscience. Whether they are seen as arriving from genetic endowment or personal experience, conscience is always and inevitably visualized in terms of guilty fear. Conscience is in the service of survival. It is a mechanism to avoid punishment, retaliation, death. It is a defensive maneuver, a reluctant sacrifice of pleasure in order to buy safety. It is instigated by fear.

A true understanding of guilt was not to emerge until Freud once again returned to the concept of repression and began to evolve what was to become known as the ego ideal. In discussing self-respect, he stated that in each individual is internalized an ideal behavior by which the actual self, or ego, judges his own behavior. This, then, is the birth of a conceptual theory of true guilt, for here the anguish of guilt is in the specific sense of personal failure that occurs when we have dishonored our own internal sense of what we ought to be. It is not fear of the other, not fear of punishment, not fear at all. It is disappointment in self.

The ego ideal represents the standard of what we feel we ought to do and be. It is the comparison of "is" and "ought" that is at the heart of ethical reasoning.

It is interesting to speculate on why, despite an early recognition of the importance of guilt, it was not acknowledged as a central and coordinating mechanism of conscience until so late. The answer could indeed be related to Freud as a person as distinct from Freud as a thinker, and specifically to the nature of some of the influences in his life. Freud was a Jew, and most of the intimate circle around him, those brilliant fathers of modern-day psychoanalysis, were also Jewish. Indeed, his few non-Jewish associates were cherished by Freud because of his personal fears that psychoanalysis would be rejected as simply a form of Jewish cult. One wonders if his indulgence of Jung, as compared with his obvious intolerance for Adler, may well not be explained, at least in part, by the fact that Jung was his major link with the Christian aristocracy of central Europe. It was at one time not fashionable to talk about Freud's Jewishness, and it is interesting how little attention was paid to Jewish influences on Freud's thinking until relatively recent years.

Despite the typical "Jewish mother" jokes, and despite the fact that guilt may occupy the Jewish heart, it is not a central issue in Jewish theology. The Old Testament is so diverse and so rich, so filled with everything, that one hesitates to say it is either this or that, for surely scholars will rise to the bait and point out the deficiencies of such thinking. Nonetheless, generally speaking, we can say of the Old Testament that it presents us with a God of justice, and a primary concern for equity and justice. In the same way, we can say of the New Testament that love and guilt are at its heart. While there are more gods that inhabit the Old Testament than I would care to attempt to list (I recognize that the God of Jeremiah is not the God of Isaiah), Jehovah nevertheless is primarily associated with moral duty, with obligation and—again—with a sense of justice. It is with Christ that the god of love reaches centrality in Western religion. Paul Tillich expressed it better:

> While the Old Testament has the experience but not the notion of conscience (Adam, Cain, David, Job), the New Testament, especially Paul, has the word and the reality. Through the influence of Paul—who in this as in other cases, has introduced elements of Hellenistic ethics into Christianity—conscience has become a common concept of Christian nations in their religions as well as in their secular period. Conscience in the New Testament has religious significance only indirectly. It has a primarily ethical meaning. . . . Consequently it is not considered to be a special quality of Christians, but an element of human nature generally. In Romans II: 14–15 Paul expresses this very strongly: When Gentiles who have no law obey instinctively the law's requirements, they are a law to themselves, even though they have no law; they exhibit the effect of the Law written on their hearts, their conscience bears them witness, as their moral convictions accuse or, it may be, defend them.

And it is amazing how well the New Testament serves that concept of conscience, for it has created for us an introjectable god. Introjection is an essential, a necessity for that identification which leads to both guilt and conscience.

Jehovah, that God of righteousness, is too "big" to be swallowed. He is the father in the sky, the inheritor of the role of the ubiquitous earth mother of primitive religions. He is formless; he defies definition, let alone ingestion. But Jesus is a model introject, ready-made for incorporation. He is an ego ideal that can be visualized in man's image, in a way that man cannot visualize himself in God's image. Jesus is divine, but divinely limited. He is somehow palpable to us, a form. We can embrace Jesus, where we can only hope that we are embraced by Jehovah. Jesus is identifiable; we can incorporate him. Indeed, Christians believe they do so with each Communion. The Eucharist is but the symbolic sacrament testifying to the role that Jesus was born to play. He is the ideal ego ideal.

The Old Testament, with its dedication to justice and the survival of a people, is the religion of the law, and the law must be designed in such a way as to ensure a moral order here on earth. The moral rules of the Old Testament are, albeit with some difficulty, followable rules that are meant to be obeyed. One can live by the Old Testament, and in fact a people did so; it served not just as a moral law but the civil law for thousands of years.

The New Testament is the religion of the ideal. Ideals are meant to be aspired to, not achieved. Whereas the failures to fulfill the obligations of the law are a violation of ethical principle, the failures to fulfill the standards of an ideal are to be expected. The purpose of the ideal is to test moral life to its limit, to make one always aspire to the limits of one's potential. A Christian may attempt to live in Jesus, but it is doubtful that any Christian can live like Jesus. You are enjoined by the Old Testament to "honor thy father and mother," which admittedly is often difficult, but certainly conceivable; the injunction to "love thy enemy" is probably not possible for the majority of us. Yet we understand what it means, and it moves us away from hatred—if not to love, perhaps at least to understanding.

Jehovah has a right to be a God of vengeance. He sets standards that the good man, if he only struggles for goodness, can achieve. He has a right to be angry when his commandments are violated. Jesus must be loving and compassionate, for he sets standards no one can achieve and he tolerates the failure in appreciation of the aspiration. We revere God and we love Jesus.

Before the introduction of the concept of the ego ideal, conscience was seen as operating on an Old Testament model. Its primary emotion was guilty fear. There was an emphasis on doing the right and the good, and a fear of transgression. The internalized conscience was essentially a righteous father, always present to look benevolently on us when we behaved well and critically when we transgressed. And when we transgressed, we felt guilty fear.

With the concept of our own ego ideal, what we experience when we transgress is closer to a feeling of failure than to a sense of wrongdoing. Ironically, it is often the parent who is least punitive that produces the most guilty child. A long-suffering mother who greets a transgression with a sigh rather than a slap is capable of producing a guilt-ridden child, who, while not terrified, is just as easily controlled by this kind of intimidation. Guilt begs for punishment and is an almost unbearable emotion. It is a sense of personal failure, and, when internalized, is independent of any external judgment. Its model is aspiration to an ideal rather than obedience to an ideal code.

As Freud continued to deal with the concept of the ego ideal (1929) what emerged was a much clearer image, which emphasized the function of conscience in the responsibility of the individual to the group. This eventually led to an elaboration of a sense of social conscience via group identity. In *Group Psychology and the Analysis of the Ego* (1921), one sees Freud at the high point of his optimism about man.

Here he views the group as organic and firmly rooted in biology. It is not just by chance that this work also represents Freud's fullest concession to concepts of love and affection. In anticipation of future work, it ties identification to the process of both conscience and loving: "Identification is known to analysis as the earliest expression of an emotional tie with another person."

The fullest expression of Freud's conceptualization of conscience comes, of course, in *The Ego and the Id* (1923). Here he brings together, with minimal contradiction, the two specific concepts of conscience which concern us. He retains his earlier ideas of conscience behavior as being motivated by the fear of retaliation for wrongdoing. In that sense the introjected father is the ever-present authority figure, who sees all, knows all, and is prepared to punish all. In this use of identification we carry with us the guardians of our morality.

In the other use of introjection, he develops to the fullest the concept of an ego ideal where conscience now functions not just in terms of fear of punishment for our transgressions, but out of a sense of guilt for having failed to act in accordance with our own internalized standards as visualized in the ego ideal. Freud was to continue to wrestle with these ideas, but for the most part they were discussions to serve other needs. It remained for other distinguished psychoanalytic authors to polish and refine these views of conscience.

The crucial linkage lies in understanding that moral behavior and conscience are directly related to the process of identification which, in its turn, is directly related to the early attachment of the infant. The identified-with people will be used to help build an internalized sense of conscience, which will then be visualized, not in terms of the parents' presence or authority, but rather as an abstract system of standards and values. They will thus seem to be independent of either the child or his parents. In other words, in the beginning the child basically accedes to the demands of his parents out of fear of losing their love, or of being punished by them. The conscience at that time is experienced as a foreign entity. As the individual develops and identifications take place, the conscience, though still perceived as a whole, will no longer be experienced as a thing apart from oneself. It no longer is "something" that one fears and feels subordinated to. It is a part of our self—not an internalized "other." When we follow the dictate of conscience via this mechanism, we seem to be doing what we "want," not what some other wants, even another within us. We are acting out of aspiration, not intimidation.

Obviously the central thesis which I am now attempting to emphasize is that there are two routes to good and unselfish behavior. We behave in socially approved manners even though it brings us in conflict with selfish interest or desire, first, out of fear of punishment (often visualized as an internalized father whom we carry within us and who is prepared to make us pay for our transgressions against the moral principles and values). This is the mechanism dominated by guilty fear. Secondly, however, we internalize a model of goodness which may arise from a parent or an idealization of the parent, but once incorporated becomes a sense of ourselves—our better half, if you will. This is our ego ideal. It is the way we would like to be. It is the person we feel we ought to be and it is the standard by which we measure ourselves. When we fail this internalized ideal, we feel we have betrayed ourself. We have done an injustice to that which we might have been and to that which we would like to be. What we feel then is not fear but guilt. Both aspects of conscience enter into unselfish behavior and acts of kindness and into that which is lumped together as "caring"; but they are different mechanisms, enhanced or diminished by a different set of experiences.

At this point it might make more sense to turn away from

the theoretical argument and examine a specific case, a case in which a misunderstanding of the nature of social behavior led to incomplete conclusions and inadequate solutions. During the height of adolescent rebellion, in the period of campus crisis, the specific relationships between the nature of the authority figures and the action of rebellious students tended to be ignored. It was particularly distressing to find even the psychoanalysts concerned paying so little heed to the concepts of ego ideals and models. It is part of the problem of psychoanalysis that, bound to a therapeutic model, it has been less willing to involve itself as directly in social problems as it has a moral responsibility to do. At any rate, in those days when there was thought to be a "crisis in authority," the academic community responded with more indignation than insight.

Conflicts with authority, rebellion, and defiance are traditionally approached by behavioral scientists from the point of view of the authority. This is no more than logical, since most people approach most problems from their own point of view. The method, then, is usually to examine the rebel rather than the state of affairs about which he is rebelling. Furthermore, the seek-and-thou-shalt-find principle, which applies in all psychological research, guarantees that "pathology" will be discovered wherever it is looked for. Since in each individual there is an abundance of dynamic factors to explain both pathological and normal behavior, it is those factors which support the *a priori* bias of the investigator that are usually marshaled to prove one's case. The equating of "psychodynamic" with "psychopathologic" is a fallacy which all psychoanalysts warn themselves against but too many succumb to. The fact that a piece of behavior is dynamically determined does not mean that it is sick. Psychodynamics are also the root of normal behavior. If there are psychodynamic reasons why I behave foolishly in a given case and do something harmful to myself, there must also be psychodynamic factors to explain why someone else in that situation behaves intelligently and to his own benefit. In addition, the nature of the causes that are elicited by any research will also be predetermined by the nature of the areas researched. Anyone digging in a potato patch will find —potatoes!

For entirely other reasons, as well, psychoanalysis in particular has tended to reinforce the social need to define rebellion in terms of the problem of the rebels. It is a field which is traditionally individual-oriented and internally directed, so it is only natural that when confronted with an act of social defiance, psychoanalysis should analyze the act. That is what is does best. But after *The Ego and the Id*, a new potential direction for analysis of rebellion occurs. Since Freud had stated that: "Social feelings rest on the foundation of identification with others on the basis of an ego ideal in common with them," we can look to the presence or absence of commonly shared values. We can examine the social structure to see what it offers the developing individual.

"The superego arises as we know from an identification with the *father regarded as a model*," Freud stresses. It may be necessary, therefore, to look to the availability of external models suitable for introjection. The possibility surely exists that, if there is a breakdown of authority, the failure may be that of the society or the parent as well as the rebel.

In the chapter on identification we have seen how often researchers stressed that a groundwork must be laid for identification through love and caring. The presence of parents, or surrogates, worthy of identification must be presented to the child. Having stated this, one need not abandon the role of fear and compliance, the power struggle, as determinants of youthful obedience or rebellion; nor does it mean that the internalized structure of the rebel is not still a source of inestimable value in understanding the breakdown of social behavior. It merely suggests that the interface between society and the individual, and the nature of the social roles of parents and other authority representations in the larger society, are also crucial factors.

I am not, of course, specifically alluding here to the violence epitomized by urban gangs. The problem of the alienated ghetto adolescent is a complex story with multiple derivatives. Economic explanations, the only kind generally offered by most sociologists, will never suffice to explain the teenager who mutilates and murders with conscienceless ease. The phenomenon of casual violence often as gratuitous as it is vile is not, and never has been, totally explicable in terms of economic deprivation. The symbolic meaning of that deprivation in the midst of promise, the sense of alienation from the world of privilege, is one possible bridge to the dissociation that allows for brutality without remorse, but there are numerous other factors. The fact that psychoanalysis has neglected its own potential for insight into this desperate social problem is to its professional shame.

I have already discussed how the abandonment of religious models, the role of the upwardly mobile society, and some of the problems of the technological state have played their part in an attrition of respectable models that leads to rootlessness and rebellion. Here, again, the inordinately prolonged dependency of human beings will play a pivotal role. This prolonged dependency is a biological fact essential to the evolution of the kind of species that we are. Capable of technology, we need the prolonged nurture and care required by any animal that has so much to learn, and requires for that learning process the evolution of its elaborate nervous system.

Prolonged dependency has facilitated the development of a technological and scientific society. Ironically, that very society, once created, will make new demands for an extension of the period of dependency beyond even those original biological limits. To become a neurosurgeon requires a greater period of learning before achieving adult, economic independence than to be a hunter.

While a child is expected to be like the parents in certain ways, there are other ways in which he is genetically and socially conditioned to distinguish himself from his parents; that is, there are prerogatives reserved for the parent and denied to the child. These are particularly magnified when "childhood" is extended far beyond the biological age where adulthood was intended. The human male is biologically fit, ready, willing, and at his most able sexually at ages twelve to seventeen in the flush of his pubescence and post-pubescence. He is obviously not capable of taking the current sociological role of parent or adult when he is sixteen or seventeen. This biological capability had, in a simpler society, a certain congruence with the social and economic responsibilities a person faced. But in our own time, particularly for the male wage-earner, the postponement has become downright ridiculous. For example, the average age of certification for a child psychoanalyst is forty-six! We may have created a kind of monster "child-adult," and this may explain some of the current dissatisfactions and disaffections of the student generation.

I can well understand why someone would be unwilling to defer the prerogatives that are reserved for adulthood to age forty-six or thirty-six or even twenty-six. Since a student is not seen as an adult, the term "student" has come to have a pejorative connotation. It implies "dependent." In addition, the male student also suffers from other expectations of a male-oriented society. To be dependent, in such a society, means to be not masculine as well as not adult. Neither of these situations is conducive to the kind of self-respect that is necessary for proper functioning. Self-respect and self-value is, as we have seen, one of the props of social behavior and responsibility to the group. While it is not the purpose here to explore these subjects in detail, I do think that there may be alternative paths to independence. It might, for example, simply be necessary to redefine the role of "student" by making it a form of career and paying one for this career, thus establishing an independent profession. The Talmudist was so treated in the Jewish ghetto communities of Europe. It may well be that much of the turmoil we define as "adolescent behavior" is a cultural artifact rather than a biological phenomenon.

What I am suggesting is that the real failure in our time may not be in the capacity of the young to identify, but in the systematic destruction of worthwhile or even identifiable models. Rebelliousness is, of course, not always a crisis or neurosis. The modest middle-class rebellions, which anyhow now seem to be abating, may have been healthy. Some of the specific rebellions made no particular logical sense at the time they were taking place; but even they may have been preferable to the self-destructive ennui, the autistic embracing of drugs, the passive narcissism that characterize part of the middle-class youth.

We have deprived middle-class youth of more than acceptable models or ideals of behavior; we have deprived them of ideals of themselves. We offer these youths little opportunity for service and giving. Affluence, coming after poverty, is seen as allowing for self-indulgence and self-gratification. Self-denial and sacrifice are seen as the punishments of poverty, rather than the privilege of abundance. We deny our youth the pleasure of self-sacrifice, of unselfishness. To give and give up, to do for others, is testament to ourselves of our worth and our strength. To deny the young the privilege of service is to deny them the pride of maturity.

I see no evidence that the young have lost their capacity to identify with authority. If anything, I see that capacity enlarged, like any need that is frustrated. The leading danger is not their rebelliousness, but their *hunger* for authoritarian figures which leads them to worship at all sorts of peculiar shrines. Each year produces a new savior, and I, personally, despair of following that long, Laing trail a-winding from McLuhan to Sufi, from macrobiotics to megavitamins, from artificial highs to natural foods, from alpha waves to Zen Buddhism, from Coke to "coke." And I visualize with fear the explosive potential for exploitation that exists, given a charismatic leader with public promises and private purposes.

In every area, with every new evidence of transgression, brutality, lawlessness, and deterioration of public safety, the first response is to increase the punishment. The assumption is always that fear is the mechanism to instill order. I do not deny the importance of fear. Nor am I lost in some liberal assumption that the justice system is designed to serve the offender. It is designed to serve the public, and if punishment and fear of retribution were the essential means of establishing law and order, it would be warranted—provided, of course, that it was not so punitive that it defined a society not worth saving.

But fear is only half the lesson and half the mechanism. There must be identification with the group, with society, with its values, with its institutions, to ensure the public safety. Instead of new methods of enforcement of obedience and fear, what is most required is a reexamination of the process of identification and pride.

We do not do harm, not calculated gratuitous harm, to our own. We do not soil our own nests. Of course, for some there is no "own." There is no identity, no group. But for most this is not true. It is merely from the mainstream of society that they are alienated. The streets of suburbia are well tended because they are "our" streets. The streets in slum neighborhoods are often not. This is an alienated population, forced to live in an alien world; it is not their street, and they have no identification with it. The garbage is in the street not just because there is poorer service there, although God knows that is true, but also because slums create slum manners and slum mentality, and these are in turn capable of creating slums.

Again, I do not want to minimize the humiliating and debilitating effects of poverty and deprivation. But what the alienated minority is deprived of is more than its equal share of material goods. That could be tolerated; there are poor societies in which the mean is incredibly lower than our minimum. What is necessary is an equal share of pride and power. For this we must replace the sources of alienation with the processes of identification. To respect (or love) others, one must respect one's self. To respect one's self, one must feel respected by others.

Obedience may be established through fear and terror, but often at such an extreme that the society is a nightmare not worthy of preservation. Social order is best protected by citizens who care. We must see our environment as part of ourselves. We must identify with our community and our neighbors. We must feel with them and for them. We must care.

CHAPTER IX

Feeling

The individual is charged by nature to survive. He has a genetic obligation to himself to grow and mature, to secure safety, and to cling to life. He also has a genetic obligation to ensure the survival of the species. Individual and group survival, although they often seem in conflict—indeed, are often brought into conflict—are inextricably linked. The group only exists by the survival of the individuals and the individual exists only in the matrix of the group.

The purposes of both forms of survival are served by built-in mechanisms—some conscious, some unconscious—of physiology, instinct, drive, and emotion. We are most aware of personal survival. It is served by fear and anger, lust and passion. We tend to serve group survivals unconsciously and without awareness of that design. Conscience and guilt serve that group purpose. They drive us, often to our own amazement, beyond selfishness and pleasure. But there are mechanisms for group survival beyond conscience. There is a kind of giving that is not self-sacrificing, but that produces pleasure and joy. And such giving is served by a different form of identification, where we identify or empathize with the small and helpless rather than the strong and capable; it is a basic mechanism in the structure of group survival. This represents an expansion of empathy beyond its usual transiency or momentary character into a steadily maintained, ongoing state of feeling.

The kind of identification previously discussed in Chapter VII is obviously a part of the process of becoming. It explains how the child moves from a stage of primary narcissism, the only time when he is truly an individual (or at least deludes himself into thinking so), to an adult stage where he will be a member of the community of supporting individuals. He will build both his maturity and his sense of conscience on his identification.

But what of that form of instantaneous identification that the parent has with the child? Obviously it does not serve the same purpose in the growth and development of the adult, and, while sharing certain features with the learning experience of the child, it must be different. Identification downward, if you will, has different mechanisms and somewhat different meanings from identification upward.

If again we take the model of mother and child, the same two stages that distinguish attachment and identification can be applied here. Stage one in the relationship of the mother to her newborn child has the same reflexive and innate appearance as the automatic attachment behavior of the infant. Of course, here it has less automaticity. We are not talking about a newborn. We are dealing with individuals who have had the opportunity to modify their genetic potential through half a lifetime of experience. Modification can mean eradication, even of reflex. Remember that all genetic determinants are determinants in name only. The genes define our potentials, which may be altered *in utero*, and undoubtedly will be after birth. Certainly, the complexity of organized social behavior is the most amenable to modification.

The nature of the species demands protective adults. We teleologically assume that an adult who has been allowed to progress through a culture that is not so distorted as to destroy all of the survival-sustaining mechanisms built into the human organism will generally develop into an adult who will routinely, and therefore genetically, respond with caring gestures, solicitude, and love to the helpless child. That much of this has a reflex quality is again demonstrated in the intriguing work of Klaus and his group, who had the imagination while examining the premature babies in their care to also examine the reflex responses of the mother. Their studies showed that there apparently were built-in patterns of behavior that the parents of newborns demonstrated, particularly in the method of holding, touching, and eye-to-eye contact.

An orderly progression of behavior is observed in mothers who are presented their infants immediately after birth. They start with fingertip touch on the infant's extremities, but within a short time, move directly to massaging the entire trunk with full palm contact. Mothers of even normal premature infants, however, are not usually presented the babies until after the first few days. These mothers followed the same course but at a much slower rate and with a lower statistic of conversion to full caressing. The early deprivation of the mother, that is, her inability to have postpartum physical contact with her child, significantly affected her behavior toward that child in such measurable means as the capacity to hold the baby in an *en face* position. And her demonstrative, stroking, and caring attitude varied from the normal even long after the birth.

> The control group comprised those who had contact with their babies that is routine in American hospitals (a glance at their baby shortly after birth, a short visit six to twelve hours after birth for identification purposes, and then twenty to thirty minutes for feeding every four hours during the day). The extended contact group consisted of mothers who in addition to the contact mentioned above were given their naked babies in bed with a heat panel for a period of one hour within the first three hours after birth and were allowed five extra hours with their baby for each of the first three days—a total of sixteen hours more than the control group.

The distinction between the two groups at one month, as judged by a group of observers who had no awareness of which parents were members of which group, was significant.

The distinctions that persisted at one year were astonishing. Mothers in the extended-contact group not only picked up their babies more often when they cried; they also tended more frequently to stay at home and provide primary care for their infants.

By one year, many of the mothers in both groups had returned to work or school. Yet "only one of the [seven] control mothers said that she missed her baby, while five of the six mothers in the extended contact group said that they worried about, or greatly missed, their baby. Six of the seven mothers in the control group did not mention the baby at all, but responded with more self-focused answers, such as: I was happy to be back at work, but I was on my feet all day."

In addition, during the physical examination of the baby, half of the extended-contact mothers spent almost the entire time at the tableside assisting the physician, while only two of the mothers in the control group did so. Indeed, half of the control mothers spent most of the time away from the examining table—seemingly bored or uninterested! When the baby cried, the majority of the control mothers spent less than a quarter of the time soothing them as did the other mothers. The mothers in the extended-contact group spent much more time soothing and were more likely to kiss their babies.

All this was consistent with the findings at one month with these same parents, that fondling and *en face* feeding of the baby was three to five times as common in the extended-contact group. Interestingly enough, in more complicated interrelationships between the two, no significant differences were found. So it was only in basic touching, fondling, eye contact, and soothing aspects that the early contacts seemed to trigger or release reactive behavior.

While this is preliminary work, it is consistent with other findings in higher animals, and does at least strongly suggest the innate and reflexive nature of certain caring behavior which would automatically be triggered in traditional, pre-cultural procedures of childbirth.

This, then, can be seen as the maternal equivalent in many ways of the traditional grasping, nuzzling, following, attachment procedures of the infant; it may require no set pattern of conditioning to emerge, merely the avoidance of impediments placed in the way of its development. There are other examples, in other contexts, of a kind of quick and fixed reflexive response triggered by physical contact that implies a capacity to identify with another in an empathetic and caring way. I have already cited the almost contagious quality of tears—totally independent of our knowledge of the context in which the tears arise in the other person's eyes. Another example is the almost uniformly stereotyped reflexive response to infants and, for that matter, to puppies or kittens.

In some individuals, the expression of any emotion has been so severely constricted by cultural demands, or simply cultural values, that they are incapable of manifesting emotions. But this absence of outward display does not necessarily imply an absence of emotion. A few years ago, back to back on the evening news on television, there were presented two particularly poignant and related scenes. Both involved the mass burial of children. In one, children who had died in an Arab attack on an Israeli school bus were mourned with massive expressions of grief, wailing, crying, and other obvious signs of physical distress in facial expression and motor behavior. In the other example, the victims of a landslide in Wales were mourned with stoic faces and silent tears. The demonstrative parents would undoubtedly have seen the response of the stoic parents as cold, heartless, and unloving. The stoic parents would have viewed the public display of emotion as a sign of indulgence, concern for self rather than occupation with the dead child. Both would be incorrect. The distinctions in response were in no way indices of grief or concern. Each group was behaving according to the dictates of its culture. Typically in many Mediterranean cultures, it is in the public expression of emotion that one pays tribute to one's love; whereas in the more northern traditions, the containing of emotion is seen as honoring it.

Some individuals, however, beyond the cultural limits, not only cannot demonstrate emotion but cannot experience it. Peculiarly, these most emotionally restricted people often have a capacity to feel emotions in the most trivial of arenas —often to their own bewilderment. It is a common observation in psychoanalytic practice that such a patient to his own chagrin may describe that while he felt unmoved by the plight of his child in an illness, he could get choked up at a sentimental scene in a tacky television play even while recognizing that the play was tacky, or experience a welling of emotion at the passing of the flag.

Little has been done to explore this distinction between true sentiment and sentimentality, but evidence seems to indicate that the capacity for sentimentality is in many people a safe substitute for the experiencing of emotion. In artificial ways, unrelated to true life and the dangers and vulnerability of true relationships, one can experience parallels of attachment, identification, and love. One wonders at the capacity of reserved people for getting involved with animal causes and in animal tales. I think of the recent popularity of that not-so-distant relation of *Peter Rabbit* called *Watership Down*. Stripped of the animal identities, it is a rather tedious adventure story, repetitive in form, predictable in outcome. True, it supplies many interesting details of rabbit life; but it may also be that an Anglo-Saxon culture which esteems self-control in human relationships is particularly vulnerable to emotional release via animal counterparts. (On the other hand, it may simply be that I as an observer have never found magic in rabbit tales.)

Stage one, then, in adult identification downward may be seen as automatic and transient reflexive behavior. This response to the helpless, the innocent, and the young can be seen as roughly equivalent to the automatic attachment behavior of the infant to his parent. So, too, can the true identification downward be related to true identification in children. This is the more involved, and again unconscious, total absorption of the child by the adult into his self-interest and self-identity mechanism. Here, too, the limitations imposed by the psychoanalytic method, which essentially detaches a person from his environment, are most strongly felt. With the infant, at least, we can go and directly observe, utilizing our psychoanalytic insights, while adapting the methodology of the behaviorists, sociologists, developmentalists. We are not, however, generally welcomed into the adult household to observe the parents' reactions to their children. The only true opportunity for such direct observation is in the postpartum period, where we have the built-in rationalization of studying the child.

Obviously, the downward identification serves different purposes, and affects different areas of functioning. The identification of the child was seen as a bridge to establishing self-confidence and the security necessary to explore the world about him. This, in turn, was part of a chain of development which will expand his environment, increase his courage and confidence in himself, help him to cope with situations, and ultimately to become the executor of his own fortunes and—at least in part—the designer of his future. The identification of the parent with the child normally serves none of these purposes. There is a distorted kind of adult identification, wherein the child is seen as an extension of one's self for purposes of fulfilling one's own frustrated needs or, in a child of the opposite sex, for being that which one's partner failed to be. For the most part, though, those are seen as negative aspects and we rebuke the parent who demands that his child vicariously gratify his own frustrated desires.

With the typical, and more normal, identification we mean something closer to "exterojection" (were there such a word) than introjection; rather than incorporating our child, it is as though we infuse or inject our feelings into his body, so that he carries within him our sensitivities; what happens to him becomes the equivalent of its happening to us. To hurt a child or to praise a child is the surest way to antagonize or ingratiate the parent. It is in this perceptual area that the identifications are most poignant. Why then call it identification at all? Because the essential ingredient of identification is the same in both. It represents a fusion of interests and identity, so that the boundaries between self and other become, as it were, symbolically blurred. The pain and pleasure of the child are not "understood" by the parent, they are felt by the parent. It is a form of fusion which, while still not love, may be the surest sign of the presence of love.

The identification of child with parents arises over a longer period of time than the identification with the child by the parent. The child's identification relates to what he absorbs from the parent, and since his horizon is expanding quickly during maturation, he will soon find other sources from which to absorb his ideas. We see the most intense process of identification with the parents in the first part of life. With the parent, on the other hand, there is a continuing, progressive, and slower sense of identification as the growing child seems more and more the adult form that parallels the parent's own experience. In a sense, the more the parent gives, sacrifices for, relates to, and endows the child with— the greater the strength of the identification. In a good relationship, time should enhance this process. The parent will continue his identifications, and with increasing consciousness, as the child is inevitably withdrawing or repressing his.

The same duality exists in terms of the meaning of love. I am not prepared to say, as some psychoanalysts have said, that the child does not feel love for the parent, that, as Fromm writes, "for most children before the age from eight and one-half to ten, the problem is exclusively that of *being loved*—of being loved for what one is. The child up to this age does not yet love; he responds gratefully, joyfully to being loved." But I would say that if the emotion which the parent feels for the child is called love, we had best recognize that the emotion of child to parent is, if not a different thing, certainly a different *form* of the thing.

Love is, of course, an enormously complex subject and it may seem strange that in a book such as this there is no chapter on love, per se. In a sense, the entire book is devoted to one form of loving, which is why love, in itself, has not been explored. The Christian theologian Daniel Williams has stated:

> Before we go further we must look at one of the perplexities in all discussions of love, the problem of language. English has one word for love. Greek has at least four. In the vocabulary of love we can distinguish between epithemia, desire, often with the connotation of impurity or lust; eros, which is love of the beautiful, the true and the good, the aspiration for fulfillment of the soul's yearning; filia, brotherly love which can mean either the comradely and affectionate love of brother and friends, or the ethical love of neighbor; and agape, which in Greek can be used for most of the loves, but in the New Testament is the redeeming love of God.

I should like to suggest that the love up (child to parent) and love down (parent for child) are not the same thing, in the same way that identification up and down is not the same; but by suggesting this, I do not wish to denigrate either. To be not the same does not mean that one is more or less precious than the other. In many ways, the problem parallels some of the difficulties philosophers and theologians have had in attempting to fuse the various traditional uses of love in their literature. In a sense, the job has been done for me. An insightful distinction between parental love and the child's love for the parent can be deduced from the following quotation in *The Nature of Love* by Irving Singer.

In the quotation, think of "eros" as the child's attitude toward the parent, and "agape" as the parent's attitude towards the child, substituting the word "child" for "man" and the word "parent" for "God."

> . . . concepts of eros and agape are ultimately inconsistent with one another: they formulate attitudes wholly divergent, necessarily irreconcilable. . . . "Eros is acquisitive desire and longing—agape is sacrificial giving. Eros is an upward movement—agape comes down. . . . Eros is egocentric love, a form of self-assertion of the highest, noblest, sublimest kind—Agape is unselfish love, it 'seeketh not its own,' it gives itself away. Eros seeks to gain its life . . . Agape . . . dares to 'lose it.' . . . Eros is determined by the quality, the beauty and worth, of its object; it is not spontaneous, but 'evoked,' 'motivated'—Agape is sovereign in relation to its object, and is directed to both 'the evil and the good'; it is spontaneous, 'overflowing,' 'unmotivated.' Eros *recognizes* value and loves it—Agape loves, and *creates value* in its object."

If we leave the principal example of the parent-child relationship, we can find other areas of identification in adults. Because of the security of the adult in his environment, because he has a lifetime history of reminiscences on which to draw, because he is adept at symbolism and metaphor, he is capable of forming partial and ready "identifications" with situations, aspects, colleagues, and even strangers whom he encounters only in passing and from a distance. This partial identification—known as empathy—has an ephemeral quality which distinguishes it from true identification. The capacity for empathy is exploited in theater, the arts, and advertising. It is also the reason why a description of thousands of deaths from an earthquake rarely "touches us" the way the description of the death of a child in our local newspaper does. We do not empathize as well with groups of people. We may be awed or "moved" by the magnitude of the disaster, but we are touched by what we can symbolically incorporate into our identification systems with those we love. In this sense empathy is also a form, albeit transient, of adult identification.

We can also, of course, identify with a group visualized as a symbolic entity or whole. That facility may explain in part some of the passion for professional sport. In the humdrum world of mediocrity that most men occupy, the capacity for vicarious excellence and achievement may seem all that is available. The theater of sports allows us to transcend the confines of the small world of nine to five, of routine and boredom, of limited pain but predictable pleasure, and enter the agony and triumph that the perfectionism of the professional affords. He does what we would do, but can't, and pretends to do it for us.

Adult identifications even on these brief levels must be with people who are identifiably like us. This is what permits group identifications, and even proximal identifications with lower forms. As I suggested earlier, it is easy to identify with the baby seal because its furry, cuddly, small-featured face somehow or other evokes the sense of an infant child. The infant cockroach, as much in the primacy of its life as the seal, evokes no such warmth or compassion. Identification of someone or something else as being like the self is remarkably broad because of the variability of the human species. We can take someone half our size, long-haired, short-haired, with different-colored eyes, of a different age, different sex, different culture, and still recognize our kinship. It permits us to identify with a large spectrum of dissimilar people—to find kinship, for example, as Americans.

Erich Fromm tends to see love in this way, not as a label descriptive of the relationship between one and a loved object, but rather as the main modality used in dealing with rootlessness and isolation. "The basis for our need to love lies in the experience of separateness and the resulting need to overcome the anxiety of separateness by the experience of union." Love, for him, is an activity; a means of self-expression and a means of attachment to a group; a fusion with one's kind. In this sense, he is dealing with Aristotelian "filia."

The peculiarities of our group identification defy logic. Why is it that we can ignore monstrous differences in size and not differences in skin color? It is part of the problem in group identification that by identifying some as being part of "us," we identify the rest as being "other." Mark Twain summed this up in a six-word dialogue following a steamboat explosion:

"Anybody hurt?"
"No'm, killed a nigger."

It may well be that someday when a psychoanalyst examines prejudice, he will find some of these answers. We know that we define the "us" as being the group with whom we can identify, to whom we can attach, and in whose presence there is security. The question to be answered is why the "other," the group to which we do not belong, must be seen as alien, strange, and different, and further why the alien must be seen as enemy.

After complaining of psychoanalysis's neglect of emotions, it would seem prudent (and pleasurable) to examine some of the real emotions that ordinary people talk about, but which never seem to enter the realm of analytic discourse. Two have particularly intrigued me—in their relatedness to our current subject, in the fact that they are part of the common speech and common experience of every person, and in the fact that to my knowledge they have never really been carefully evaluated in psychological studies. They are the concept of being "touched," and the entirely different experience, that of "feeling hurt." I select these two out of the number of emotional complexes that are available for virgin analysis because they obviously relate, at different ends of the spectrum, to concepts of caring and identification.

With emotions there is a sloppiness in public usage that follows closely on the difficulty of definition. People know how they feel and assume that others feel the same. Communication need only be suggestive, and so the language of emotion is imprecise to the point of making generalization hazardous. Nonetheless, it is worth making a beginning.

To be touched by something is closely related to being moved by it, and may be a subheading under that broader category. We are, however, most likely to reserve being touched for specifically human relationships. We are touched by the thoughtfulness of a friend; we are touched by a kindness, an unexpected service, or the observation of such; by acts of courtesy, decency, humanity, warmth, generosity, love. Being touched is almost exclusively used in terms of the way one is treated by others. Of course, with our capacity to empathize and identify, the treatment need not be directed toward us.

When we are moved, it may often be by a scene of great natural beauty, by a musical phrase, by an image of poetry that even when obscure in its literal meaning reaches some awareness beyond cognition. To be moved is generally a more profound emotion, and when we say that we are moved by acts of others, it transcends the literal action of the specific event and tends to have a more universal meaning for us. To be touched is to be made to feel good within our relationships. To be moved is to be made to feel good beyond our relationships. It is a transcendental experience that projects us above experience. If we are moved by a loving act it will be because it exposes us not just to being loved, but to awe at the concept of love.

We are touched when we experience, either directed toward us or in abstraction, the caring and loving acceptance of others. It is an unexpected kindness from an unexpected source that catches us up with emotion and "touches" us. We use the term more often in relationship to the distant person than the close; we are touched more often by the expression of caring from the near-stranger or stranger. Its presence in loved ones is expected and assumed. If a stranger offers us a part of his lunch where food is scarce, a lift when needed, we are touched; when a mother does these things, it is an unnoticed part of the tacit loving arrangement. When we are touched by those we love, and with whom we have our principal identification, it is more often than not in an unexpected situation which then revives the deeper emotions of love. It is the pleasurable sense or surprise of being cared for.

We are left, however, with the question of why we use the tactile sense for this metaphor. To use again the analogy with the emotion that was not analyzed, it seems easy to understand why we talk about being moved. It is usually in transcendental experiences that we speak of being moved, and we will have a sense of literally being lifted up out of ourselves. But why touched?

> The greatest sense in our body is our touching sense. It is probably the chief sense in the process of sleeping and waking; it gives us our knowledge of depth or thickness and form; we feel, we love and hate, are touchy and are touched through the touch corpuscles of our skin.

It is with this quote from J. Lionel Taylor that Ashley Montagu opens his book, *Touching, The Human Significance of the Skin*. In this opening chapter, he points out not only the importance of skin contact and stimulation in lower animals and in the human species, but also its remarkable neglect by social scientists, poets, psychiatrists, and other students of human behavior. The amount of tactile stimulus that is given to early mammals is surprising. Still more surprising, however, is the dependence on such stimulation for the inception of basic life-sustaining physiological processes. The relationship of the licking of the perianal region with the inception of proper urinary function has previously been referred to. Self-licking in preparation to giving birth is also an essential phenomenon. When pregnant rats are prevented from licking themselves, the mammary glands develop about 50 per cent below the normal. Other studies are reported which document the fact that physical contact is essential to the establishment of brooding. Montagu notes that: "Stimulation of the skin apparently constitutes an essential condition in causing the pituitary gland to secrete the hormone most important for the initiation and maintenance of broodingness, namely prolactin. This is the same hormone associated with the initiation and maintenance of nursing in mammals, including the human mother." One can add to this evidence the previously cited fact that the stroking behavior of mothers is one of the two or three primary functions of attachment in early life; the personal experience of what stroking means in caring situations; and our knowledge of how important skin contact is in sexual loving.

With all of this, it is incredible how little attention has been given to touching. Nonetheless the language of the common man accepts the importance of the skin. After all, the two distinct and separate meanings of the word "feeling" bind the skin to our entire emotional life. It is to Montagu that I am indebted for the intriguing fact that feeling "is by far the longest entry—fourteen full columns—in the magnificent Oxford English Dictionary." It may be that, again, methodology determines interest in, and therefore the ultimate importance of, any subject. Perhaps it was when psychiatrists eschewed the laying on of hands that they lost touch with the importance of the organ of the skin.

"Hurt," of course, means pain or injury, but when we say that we "feel hurt" we leave the realm of the physical and enter into psychological phenomena. Here, too, it means pain, but of a very special kind and a special intensity. Obviously, to feel hurt does not carry with it the burden of anguish. The latter immediately implies a depth of mental pain; hurt suggests slight injury, or better still, a slight.

One can, of course, feel "deeply hurt," but that only supports the notion that hurt is more normally used in a more superficial way. "Hurt" again, like "touched," is almost inevitably associated with the response to an action of another person. We are not hurt by the fact that it rains on our parade.

In all, "hurt" carries with it the connotation of being slighted, neglected, unloved, uncared for, and unappreciated. If we are generally touched by behavior that does more for us than we might have expected, we are hurt by behavior that does less for us than we feel we have a right to expect. It is my feeling that in most senses of the usage, being touched and feeling hurt are polar phenomena. I am touched by your solicitude and hurt by your lack of solicitude; touched by the fact that despite a limited acquaintance, you remembered my birthday; hurt by the fact that even though you are my spouse, you had forgotten. If being touched is preeminently visualized in terms of the delighted and somewhat unexpected caring attitude of an individual, feeling hurt is the absence of such an attitude where we feel entitled to it and where we have every reason to expect it. In that sense we can see where we are more likely to be hurt by those who are close to us and touched by casual friends. In both cases there is an unexpected and unwarranted quality. Those who know us slightly honor us with their affection or attention, as those who know us well abuse us by failing to show that they care. To feel hurt occurs with a failure in caring. This, then, represents our vulnerability through attachments, our need to feel cared for. It is interesting that we are the most likely to feel hurt by a tact ("touch")-less statement from a loved one.

To feel "slighted," of course, is closely aligned, and probably warrants an investigation of its own. It is used somewhat differently from hurt and is more tightly bound to *its* root, that of being made to feel small, small almost to the point of invisibility, and therefore to be neglected. While we can also be hurt by neglect, it must then have an implication of distancing from expected love.

All of the discussion of touching can be understood as the other end of the pole from being hurt. The fact that the two words draw from such different roots is also, I think, not insignificant. To be treated kindly by someone who is not a primary caretaker is like a stroke or a caress. It is unnecessary, but a delight. To be neglected by someone who should be in a caring position has the implication and the potential for real damage. We feel pleasure and contact in the former, but we feel injury in the latter. Approval from a stranger is a luxury; care from a loved one may be a matter of survival. Being touched, then, is the awareness of an unexpected identification with us—a sign that someone cares who need not. Hurt is the absence of such caring and identification from one who ought to be displaying them.

These are two examples from the quiet end of that vast spectrum of human emotions. The emotional range of human beings is so far beyond what is present in other forms of life as to constitute a new dimension of response. Such feelings refine our pleasures, and define our pains. They are adjuncts to our intelligence and imagination in guiding our behavior —part of that complex of adaptive mechanisms that substitutes for the fixed and automatic response mechanisms of lower forms and allows for variability and spontaneity. They make us incredibly more adaptable than if our behavior were genetically predetermined. Where other species will die with drastic environmental changes or survive only through mutant forms, we can accommodate within our species.

Our feelings and our intelligence guide us through the subtle range of possibilities that exist for us between fight and flight. It is our adaptability that makes us supreme survivors.

CHAPTER X

Despair

When individuals feel sufficiently unwanted and unloved—when they feel abandoned by those whom they love —they may slip into the most dangerous and painful of psychological states, a depression. Indeed, for many years, depression and abandonment were inextricably linked in psychoanalytic theory.

Depression falls into that category of clinical phenomena which would also include nightmares, traumatic war neuroses, and repetitive painful activity and are baffling because of their perversely nonadaptive, or at least maladaptive, quality. Why should someone opt for painful behavior? Why should someone cling to self-recrimination, self-reproach, misery, and unhappiness? Almost every behavioral theory assumes the hedonic principle. It is "unnatural" for someone to embrace pain rather than pleasure.

Early attempts to understand depression made the key comparison between grief and depression. Obviously, there is a relation between the two. The melancholic and the mourner look alike, they are sufferers, their reactions are in many ways similar. Yet, mourning is assumed to be a normal phenomenon of human behavior. One does not think of sending an individual to a psychiatrist because he is mourning the death of a loved one. But depression seems to be grief gone haywire—extended, excessive, often unprecipitated and seemingly unwarranted. Some mourners do go beyond the normal period of grief into an extended and profound de-

pression. On examination, these individuals often demonstrate a marked ambivalence about the loss of the loved one.
It was early recognized that an individual is likely to pass
over the bounds of grief into depression when his reaction
to the lost love is charged with anger as well as love. It is well
to remember here that what is meant by "depression" is not
what the layman visualizes. It is not the "down" feeling that
one calls "being depressed," but rather that clinical concept
sometimes called psychotic depression in which an individual
is paralyzed with grief and despair; often suicidal; and with
a clear-cut set of symptoms that sharply distinguishes it from
grief.

The mourner and the depressed person do share certain
phenomena. There is that feeling of blueness that we all
associate with depression, a deflated, down mood. There is
also a withdrawal of interest in the outside world, a marked
inhibition of activity, and a loss of capacity to love. But in
addition to these, the depressed patient shows certain other
features which take him beyond grief. Specifically, there are
clusters of feelings about himself which seem particularly
masochistic; a deflation of self-esteem encouraged by the
individual; an obsessive self-accusation; and often a delusional
need for self-punishment.

Early psychoanalytic concepts explained depression by
utilizing the concepts of introjection and identification. That
same sense of identification central to survival, essential for
a sense of self and a sense of self-worth, perversely seems to
serve to debase ourselves. The idea was that the depressed
patient, threatened by the loss of a loved object, incorporated
that object into himself in a desperate attempt to cling to
it. At the same time his ambivalence is acted out on the
image of that object, which is of course now fused with
the self. The self-deprecatory and self-abusive behavior of the
depressed patient represent the confusion in identity between him and the lover he is trying to retain through
introjection. This complicated concept saw the depressed

individual as almost delusionally punishing the abandoning figure within himself.

What one sees here, obviously, is a rudimentary anticipation of the yet-to-be-developed concept of the superego. The discussion in our chapter on conscience, while appearing earlier in this book, is of course a much later development of Freud's and drew extensively from this original work on depression. Conscience, too, can lower self-esteem, produce self-accusation, establish a need for self-punishment. Conscience, too, seems if not self-destructive, at least not serving the purposes as Freud understood them of human motivational drive. If all normal purposes are in the expressions of instinctual pleasure, then conscience is also not self-serving. This is a limited and isolated view of conscience and man.

More careful examination, however, indicates that a very special kind of person tends to fall into a depression following a mourning period. Those persons who are predisposed to depression have an intense craving for approval and love; and are persons who have, in addition to the anguish of loss and the rage over loss, a significant measure of guilt. The self-punitive behavior, so central to depression, can then be seen as an expiatory act for the often repressed and unconscious sense of anger. The self-abusive behavior of the depressed patient may merely be the berating of conscience. In this view, guilt, atonement, and forgiveness are seen as the key dynamic in depression.

So far, the one feature common to all early theories of depression presented had been the implicit equation of grief and melancholy. It was this analogy that dictated the central role of the "lost love object" in the etiology of depression. Unfortunately, theoretical brilliance is not always congruent with validity. There are numerous examples in medicine where a wrong theory has been perpetuated far beyond any reasonable point because of the intellectual elegance of its formulation and the reputation of its author.

Obviously, clinical experience indicated that depression was not always initiated by the loss of a loved object. Rather than carefully examining the other initiating factors to test for an alternative hypothesis, it was assumed that the seeming alternative precipitants must be merely "symbolic" representations of the lost love.

In my first dealings with depressed patients, I was impressed that not one of the suicidal patients I examined made such attempts because of the breakup of a love affair. It began to seem strange that people responded preponderantly more to the representation of the fact than to the fact itself. In retrospect, the bias became obvious. In those early days I was in a veteran's hospital and saw only male patients. When I began to see women patients I observed that, indeed, many of them became depressed when they were rejected or abandoned in love. But what causes a man to become depressed? Almost invariably, it is a sense of personal failure, usually in a career or financial matter: he has failed, he has been fired from a job, he has been socially humiliated. A feeling of impotence and uselessness dominates his mood. I began to think that, at least in men, the reverse of what Freud had said might be true: that the love object, when it is a precipitant, must really be a symbol of something more basic. Later on I read a passage written not by a psychiatrist but a philosopher; in his essay *The Sickness Unto Death*, Kierkegaard says:

> Despair is never ultimately over the external object but always over ourselves. A girl loses her sweetheart and she despairs. It is not over the lost sweetheart, but over herself-without-the-sweetheart. And so it is with all cases of loss whether it be money, power, or social rank. The unbearable loss is not really in itself unbearable. What we cannot bear is in being stripped of the external object, we stand denuded and see the intolerable abyss of ourselves.

Here Kierkegaard, well before the time of Freud, focuses on two elements of depression that seem crucial: a sense of hopelessness and a sense of helplessness. Depression implies a lowering of spirits (often its most visible sign), but it was from Freud we learned that the visible signs or symptoms of a disease may be a side-effect rather than an etiological agent—part of the reparative process. Despair, on the other hand, suggests hopelessness, and a sense of hope lost is indeed fundamental in the causing of depression. Hopelessness in the human being is always associated with helplessness, a word we take so much for granted that we do not analyze its implications. Its literal meaning suggests that as long as there is another caring person around to *help* we are not helpless, i.e., defenseless and impotent.

Kierkegaard also suggests that it is not over the loss of another but over the depletion of ourselves that we suffer. We feel despair when our resources for coping have been diminished, and if those resources for coping are too invested in a person on whom we are dependent, then the loss of that person will precipitate depression. But similarly if we are dependent on our social position, our status, or our business, we will be vulnerable to depression with their loss.

The precipitating experience, then, in a depressed patient may be a loss of self-esteem or a loss of any supplies which are believed would secure or even enhance that self-esteem. It is not essentially the loss of the loved one or its symbolic counterparts that causes depression. Indeed, only when that loved one is too heavily invested with our self-esteem does his loss produce a depression. What we are mourning is our lost self-esteem, the loved one merely being *symbolic of it*. By extension, any loss of self-esteem or any symbol of it should produce a depression. If a man is depressed over the loss of a job, it is not because the job symbolizes a loved one but because it is his primary source of self-esteem.

The loss of the loved one is then the instrument for depression only in those dependent people who perceive, even if inaccurately, that particular loved one as an essential instrument for their survival. This is why women more frequently than men go into depression over loss of a loved one. In our culture, security generally is invested in the male role. A woman asks how she is going to live, to educate her children, make her way alone.

In addition, in a male-dominated society such as ours has been, a man was the major, often the only, prestige source available to a woman—it was her husband's position that was her vicarious pride. On the other hand, a man's pride, masculinity, and self-confidence are based primarily on his professional career and his personal attainments. More men jump out of a window because of the loss of a business than because of the loss of a child. Why? Not because they love their children less, but because in losing their businesses they lose security, prestige, self-pride, and ultimately faith and trust in themselves.

It is hoped that with the reexamination of these gender stereotypes which have dominated our society, and have caused such grief for both men and women, a reallocation of pride and esteem systems will occur, making each group less vulnerable to a sense of failure because its members have more and diverse sources for pride and success than before.

Edward Bibring, a major student of depression, added significant awareness to the understanding of what is likely to drive us to despair. It is when we are particularly tenacious in clinging to certain ambitious, adolescent goals that we are most vulnerable to that overwhelming failure that depression represents. In other words, it is the contrast of our goals with our own awareness of our helplessness to achieve them which is likely to produce depression. It is this exaggerated disparity which destroys one's confidence. The goals that are likely to get us most in trouble are: a wish to be worthy and loved; a wish to be strong and superior; and a wish to be good and loving.

The first and third are often seen as identical phenomena.

They are not. It is the cynicism of our time that sees all loving and giving only in terms of wishing for reciprocity. The truth may be quite the contrary. It is indeed "better to give than to receive" because, whereas receiving is pleasurable and satisfies certain needs, it *does* place one in the position of being a recipient, or dependent, with the potential for ego diminution implicit in that position. By contrast, there is extra joy in giving because of the sense of one's self as a giver. This is ego-enhancing.

Under his system Bibring concludes that depression stems primarily from within the ego itself, from an inner-system conflict. Can there be a totally internalized conflict when speaking of the ego? Can there be a deflation of self-esteem without the interplay of an environment? I doubt it. Is not success or failure essentially an environmentally determined phenomenon? After all, success and failure are not inborn, basic concepts. They are not even absolutes. The environment defines what success is, or failure. Thus I simply cannot conceive of an ego conflict that excludes both conscience and environmental considerations. What may be deceptive is that the individual is reacting to his personal, distorted perception of the environment. In Erikson's terms, he is responding to reality, not to actuality, by imposing on the current situation the circumstances of a previous time.

At any rate, depression is an ego reaction, and anything that lowers self-regard or -image without changing the narcissistic aims predisposes to depression. On that basis it is easy to see why one of the most common predispositions to depressions is the starting of an analysis. A patient still unconsciously bound to his grandiose plans can see analysis as a humiliating experience.

A second common stimulus to depression in the course of analysis comes with the removal of favorite illusions and the weakening of neurotic defenses. For example, the obsessive patient sees himself as accomplishing his narcissistic aims via his obsessive work habits, and when you challenge these, deglamorize them, or make them less acceptable, depression can occur.

Originally, Freud saw self-attack and diminished self-esteem as the *result* of depression, which in turn was due to the loss of a loved object. Bibring took the final position of reversing the roles and stating that diminished self-esteem is the *cause* of depression. He should have gone one step further.

It is intriguing to notice how many psychoanalysts refer to the crises in self-*esteem* when, more specifically, they are describing self-*confidence*, confidence in the operating capacity of the ego—coping, if you will. This does not mean self-esteem in terms of self-love, but rather the trust one has in one's own ego, in its ability to meet and solve problems essential to survival.

It is in paranoia that one sees a true crisis in self-esteem, with the consequent emphasis on shame and self-disgust. It is not the *lovability* but the *dependability* of self that is questioned in depressed patients. Obviously, the sense of helplessness will result in a lowered self-esteem, but this is caused by a shattered self-confidence. Self-pride and self-confidence are a different order of things from self-esteem; and while they can be derived from it, they are not inevitably derivative phenomena or inextricably linked to self-esteem. If anything, progressively we are beginning to see self-esteem as a derivative phenomenon.

There is a type of depressed patient in whom self-esteem does seem to be the paramount issue. This is the infantile and narcissistic individual who has never developed a sense of trust in the executive capacity of his ego. For him, survival is always seen in terms of infantile dependency; convinced of his weakness, he survives because of the protection of the strong and loving figures in his life. But loving figures require one to be loveworthy or lovable, and when a patient with this dynamic pattern loses his sense of self-worth, he feels he loses his loving protector and, with it, his security.

This is precisely the patient who will have a depression precipitated by the loss of a loved object. Childhood depression is characteristically of this type.

What is important to realize is that depression can be precipitated by the loss or removal of *anything* that the individual overvalues in terms of his security. To the extent that one's sense of well-being, safety, or security is dependent on love, money, social position, power, drugs, or obsessional defenses—to that extent one will be threatened by its loss. When the reliance is preponderant, the individual despairs of survival and gives up. It is that despair which has been called depression.

Hopeless and helpless, he gives up the struggle. It is this abandonment which makes depression different from other psychological conditions. The ego is paralyzed because it feels incapable of meeting life's dangers—a paralysis that is unique to depression. We are conditioned to look for the "meaning of symptoms," a meaning in terms of problem-solving. With depression, the meaning is understood in its absence of meaning. Symptoms are the attempts of the neurotic individual to compromise his way out of a conflict situation. They are the reparative maneuvers and manipulations of the threatened ego. In depression, however, the distinguishing feature is the paucity of such maneuvers. The "symptoms" are the non-symptoms of passivity, inactivity, resignation, and despair. Here the reparative mechanisms are at a minimum. The depressive is not like the phobic, who has found an illusion of safety through the mechanisms of displacement and avoidance. He has no illusions. The disease represents the bankruptcy of survival mechanisms.

What can be said of depression in its most extreme clinical form can be extended to the sense of despair in everyday life. It is a humiliating, debasing feeling, and a dangerous one. It sees one abandoned and alienated from supporting love, uncherished and unwanted; it abounds with anger, resentment, and a sense of alienation and isolation. It breaks down social communication and a sense of the self with the others, in a way that mere economic deprivation does not.

It is when deprivation is seen as stemming from indifference to us or, worse, contempt for us as individuals, that we feel isolated and alienated. It is when we feel that society does not represent an extension of ourselves; when we are found "not acceptable" into this symbolic family setting; and when we are made to feel like the "other"—then we will surely see those privileged and secure representatives of the society and the society itself as alien and other to us.

This deprivation may be tolerable if there is some pathway to privilege and approval, regardless of how tortuous and difficult. When the path is barred, however, or so obscured that it seems not present, despair can ensue, with its concomitant angers and retroflexed self-destructive rage. It can lead to the destruction of self via drugs or despair, or the destruction of others through the rage of impotence and frustration.

To be totally unaccepted, to be totally unloved, indeed, to be almost totally disapproved, either requires the rejection of one's self—an intolerable situation—or a total dissociation with the judging individual. Such total dissociation is dangerous, however, when we are required to live in that social community. Surely the kind of adolescent brutality that is evidenced in the newspapers every day, in which a street mugger hits a random woman over the head with a lead pipe as a convenient means of gaining the $6 in her purse, implies more than just the need for $6. It suggests that the concept of identity has been destroyed, or never developed; that the person now feels so "other" that he is no longer within the framework of identification necessary for introjection of a value system. Such behavior is beyond the golden rule, for that implies the identity of personhood between the other and you. Obviously it is more analogous to the squashing of a bug approaching your picnic table. To give up on one's self is to give up on one's own personal value, and ultimately to give up a sense of values.

It is always dangerous to project from the individual to the state; I shudder each time I read, for example, a psychoanalysis of "Nazism" which equates the state with a person and describes the political complex in terms normally used for a personal psychosis. But when I talk about national despair, I am not talking about social institutions as a political scientist would; I am talking about the increasing number of individuals who have lost hope and confidence, at least in the political area. In that sense, it seems to me legitimate to talk about a kind of national despair. Rollo May has said, "Care is a state in which something does *matter*; care is the opposite of apathy. . . . If we do not care for ourselves, we are hurt, burned, injured. This is the source of identification: we can feel in our bodies the pain of the child or the hurt of the adult. *Life* comes from physical survival; but the *good life* comes from what we care about."

If we are not cared for by others, we cannot care for ourselves. A society which treats any serious segment of its population, whether blacks, women, or youth, with distaste or disrespect, runs the risk of convincing that group of its own inadequacy and thus alienating it from identification with the group and allegiance to its moral codes. If we do not care for ourselves, we cannot care for others. Giuseppe Mazzini said that "we improve with the improvement of humanity; nor without the improvement of the whole can you hope that your own moral and material condition will improve. Generally speaking, you cannot, even if you would separate your life from that of humanity; you live in it, by it, for it."

Beyond the mistreated minority, a problem is emerging for the advantaged middle class. We are *all* becoming alienated from our culture. If our disillusionment with our institutions and our way of life is allowed to drift into the hopelessness of despair, we will passively embrace those features of our own potential that are the only antagonists strong enough to threaten human survival. Self-hatred and self-pity are the enemies. A denigrated self-image is a tar-baby. The more we play with it, embrace it, the more bound we are to it. Attacks on ourself and our nature are the last whimpering maneuvers before the catatonic acceptance of defeat.

CHAPTER XI

Hope

In depression *Homo sapiens*, that most resource-ful of all creatures, abandons hope in his own resources—his capacity to cope and survive. He passively awaits his pleasure-less and inevitable decline. Without struggle or desire, he is helpless. Despair is the condition which alone ensures its anticipated end.

The reasons for despair seem obvious; the reasons for hope less so. Look around and the world seems a mess. But it is neither the best of times nor the worst of times. Violence, brutality, hunger, injustice, bigotry, war, personal abuse, inequity exist in our generation as they have in all the generations in history that preceded us. One suspects less so, but takes little comfort from the fact. When one plays the game, prompted by John Rawls's discussion on justice, of selecting a time in which we would choose to live with the understanding that we cannot choose who we would be in that time or culture, there are few who would risk the fate of being the lowest in other places and other times. We tend to return, embarrassedly, to the comfort of the contemporary.

Our despair lies not in the state of the world at large, but in the failure of our aspirations and the abandonment of our dreams. We have looked at the best of us, at our most civilized, at our most progressive, and have found that it, too, seems not to work. The dream of the nineteenth cen-tury is defunct; yet we see no alternative, for that dream was based on personal glory, on a sense that our own intel-

ligence through the instruments of technology would solve
the natural problems of existence, bring us surcease from
pain, and herald a life of justice, of pleasure and pride. The
inequitable distribution of resources was depressing enough
when it was simply material good; it is particularly offensive
when it extends to the very source of survival. How can we
have sympathy for a world in which the anguish of the
hungry is paralleled by the anguish of the obese who suffer
from their self-indulgence?

It is the observation of the most successful in the most
successful of societies that is particularly depressing; it is the
joylessness of middle-class American and western European
life written about by middle-class American and western
European writers that destroys the hope which defends
against despair. Technology, even when it fulfills our aspirations, seems to betray our needs. We have been to the moon
and it is a cold place.

Certainly there has been in recent times little comfort in
the contemplation of the human spirit. When 6 million
Jewish men, women, and children were being systematically
destroyed by the countrymen of Kant, the descendants of
Mozart and Goethe, it exposed a bestiality that we knew
existed in man but dared not acknowledge. Disgust, rage,
shame, and guilt would only lead to despair, however, when
the actions of the Nazis were supported and encouraged by
the apathy of those who professed to represent the nobler
aspects of human potential. Hate is not polar to love, as
heat is to cold. Hate and love can coexist; those we love, by
the very intensity of involvement implied, are capable of
generating passions of hate. Indifference is the antonym of
love, and it was the bloodless indifference of the Christian
churches, the loveless devotees of a God of love, and the
arrogant detachment of the enlightened democracies, those
inhuman heirs of humanism, that drove us to the brink of
despair. And yet, even then, Thomas Mann was capable of
saying:

. . . today more than ever—I feel we must not, however
well founded our doubts, be betrayed into mere cynicism and
contempt for the human race. We must not—despite all
the evidence of its fantastic vileness—forget its great and
honorable traits, revealed in the shape of art, science, the
quest for truth, the creation of beauty, the conception of
justice. Yes it is true, we succumb to spiritual death, when
we show ourselves callous to the great mystery on which we
are touching when we utter the words "man" and "humanity."

It is the lack of humanity where we most rightly anticipate
its presence that crushes hope and initiates despair. It is the
lack of visible progress in the times and places where progress
is most to be expected that leads a distinguished social scientist to despair and urge that we develop pills to curb human
assertion and aggression, when he must be fully aware that
were such drugs ever to be developed, the last people they
would be used on would be political leaders, and the first
would be the deprived.

It is the gap between promise and achievement that will
even determine how we define "achievement." It is the
polarization of our society that makes particularly bitter the
deprivations. And the polarization is severe and does warrant
concern.

If the world does seem in more desperate straits than ever
before, this stems from the fact that the only solutions that
are obvious to us now (because they were solutions that
were so effective in the past) seem not to be effective any
more. Further, those very past successes that technology
achieved seem to be contributing to today's failures. We are,
for example, because of technology, moving toward a homo-
geneous small world. With all of the differences that may or
may not exist between Communist China and the United
States, the similarities and the proximities are just as apparent. When Periclesian Greece and Imperial Rome talked
about the destruction of civilization, they narcissistically

referred to their small corner of the world. We are now one small world, and we will rapidly become even smaller. When we now talk about the destruction of civilization, we mean the destruction of the world—a conceivable possibility in a way that it never was before. Contagious disease may be limited by physical contact and community boundaries, or by the broad expanse of oceans; the contagion of violence, thanks to nuclear weapons and advanced rocketry, knows no boundaries.

And so we despair, not because we are abandoned by God —it was we who abandoned Him—but because we think that we have used our best and it was not enough. We despair as a group in the same way that we despair as individuals, when we feel impotent and unable to cope. To think, however, that we have exhausted the potentials of our true technology, in other words our imagination, is preposterous. It is as though we have recognized the limitations of the balloon and not yet discovered the airplane. Our first models served us so well that we needed to explore no others. Now we know differently; we must begin to find different designs, different models, and different motives. The problems are not what we once thought they were and that is good to have discovered. For then, we seek different solutions.

Coming face to face with our increasing capacity to destroy ourselves, our kind, and indeed our world, has led many, particularly among the young, to reject not just the specific models but the generic ones. They have given up, not just on one man or one group of men, but on man himself. I see one evidence of this in the so-called right-of-nature movement. Fifty years ago, Robinson Jeffers's personal statement that he would rather kill a man than a hawk seemed idiosyncratic and bizarre; now he is part of the crowd. We hear talk that the world would be "better off" without people. To me this seems monstrous. I can understand no rational starting point for discourse among people except an anthropocentric one. I can understand the deep concern for our natural environment, but only as secondary to the needs of people. To me that environment will always be seen as a harmonious milieu which is necessary for people to become whatever their potential allows them to become. I have never seen "it" as having rights of existence beyond us. I recognize no romantic right of a sequoia to exist in splendid isolation from the purposes or perception of people. I acknowledge the anthropocentricity of this, and I suspect it may be a product of my time and training; but if man is to be completely destroyed, you may take the redwoods and the butterflies right along with him.

In this area, at least, I am in good company. George Gaylord Simpson has said:

> Even when viewed within the framework of the animal kingdom and judged by criteria of progress applicable to that kingdom as a whole and not peculiar to man, man is thus the highest animal. It has often been remarked . . . that if, say, a fish were a student of evolution he would laugh at such pretensions on the part of an animal that is so clumsy in the water and that lacks such features of perfection as gills or a homocercal caudal fin. I suspect that the fish's reaction would be, instead, to marvel that there are men who question the fact that man is the highest animal. It is not beside the point to add that the "fish" that made such judgments would have to *be* a man!
>
> Is it necessary to insist further on the validity of the anthropocentric point of view, which many scientists and philosophers affect to despise? Man *is* the highest animal. The fact that he alone is capable of making such a judgment is in itself part of the evidence that this decision is correct.

I do not despair at the state of the world; I despair at the current state of passive disenchantment and self-denigration. Given knowledge of the nature of the human being, such worry is warranted. And psychological definitions of the human state tend to be self-fulfilling prophecies. We may not be what we think we are—but what we think we are will determine in great part what we are to become. We must not design our future in terms of our disillusionment with self, for those designs, even if erroneously conceived, will influence the future development of our species. It is this that I find so frightening in the anti-person bias of so much of the back-to-nature movement; for if there is nobility in our world, it is the presence and form of people that conceptualizes that nobility, and thereby creates it.

There is no innate grandeur in a sunset; grandeur is a transcendent feeling of the human species shared by no other animal. In fact, the sun does not really set, except in human perception. Of course, the garbage in the rivers, the litter in the streets, the destruction of the forests, and the pollution of the air offend me, because they diminish the environment in which human beings live, and will thereby diminish them as human beings. To talk, however, of "what a good place the world would be if it weren't for the vile and destructive nature of man" is foolish, particularly when articulated by a member of that species. As William James points out in "The Moral Philosophy and the Moral Life":

> . . . We have learned what the words "good," "bad," and "obligation" severally mean. They mean no absolute natures, independent of personal support. They are objects of feeling and desire, which have no foothold or anchors in Being, apart from the existence of actually living minds.

> Wherever such minds exist, with judgments of good and ill, and demands upon one another, there is an ethical world in its essential features. Were all other things, gods and men and starry heavens, blotted out from the universe, and were there left but one rock with two loving souls upon it, that rock would have as thoroughly moral a constitution as any possible world which the eternities and immensities could harbor. It would be a tragic constitution, because the rock's inhabitants would die. But while they lived, there would be real good things and real bad things in the universe; there

would be obligations, claims, and expectations; obediences, refusals, and disappointments; compunctions and longings for harmony to come again, and inward peace of conscience when it was restored; there would, in short, be a moral life, whose active energy would have no limit but the intensity of interest in each other with which the hero and the heroine might be endowed.

It is not just chance that James places two people on his rock. For personhood requires relationship. In the short-term evaluation of that relationship, we view ourselves with contempt; it is a longer look that I am asking for in order to discover the hope that is defined in the essence of our species. It is the essence of our species, not just to relate but to relate with loving care. This essence we may, as with any-thing else, destroy; but we must not underestimate its strength nor how much of us it still possesses.

Each child born reaches frantically and hungrily for the caring figure who must be there for his survival even while he is unaware of her existence. The ludicrously helpless phenomenon of the human infant is testament to the bonds of love expressed in caring. This creature—designed genetically, impulsively, and instinctively to seek to attach itself symbiotically to an adult form—will find, when uncor-rupted, a reflexive, genetically determined, impulse-driven, embracing guardian of its future which is an essential part of the caring adult. From dependency to attachment, through caring, the infant will construct the confidence that enables him to separate and grow, so that even in that growth he will be able to form the new kind of fusion known as identifica-tion which will lead to love and loving. We find a way of using the best, the most loving aspects, of even imperfect parental figures to build that self-image which is necessary for us to grow into loving, caring people capable of sustain-ing the cycle of care vital for the survival of a species designed like ours. And if we despair, even that is a product of our hopes. It is the expectation of love unreceived, or the unachieved good we had hoped to do, which leads us most often to our sense of personal worthlessness or failure.

This caring nature is a fact of design. But social living is also a fact of design. We must trust ourselves and love ourselves for the primary purpose of loving others and caring for them. This extends beyond the world of the child and into the life of the adult. We do not *choose* to live in social relations; we are obliged to. In his *Animals as Social Beings*, Adolf Portmann says: "Man comes to 'sociability' not by 'arrangement,' by rational decision, but from the natural, primary disposition which he shares with all higher animals. Attraction to other members of the species precedes all hostility and repulsion; solitariness is always secondary, a flight from the natural bond."

It is this obligation to live in groups which renders the destruction of social living so dangerous, and makes a neglect of the problems of public safety by the social and behavioral scientists so distressing. Of course, the unconscionable use of those most worthy words "law and order" as a euphemism for racism was a singular factor in making the intellectuals recoil from a serious consideration of the importance of that issue. But law and order *are* both essential for group living, and group living is a requirement of our species, if we are to continue with the nature that defines our species. It *is* a concern when people can no longer walk the streets of our cities, when certain parks are declared out of bounds and no longer even patrolled by police. The answer is not in the statistics of those who have succeeded in walking the streets with safety. If an adequate percentage is reached in any series, it is sufficient unto the whole. The knowledge that only 10 per cent of an area is booby-trapped does not give me comfort in walking through that area. Along with our concern for those factors which reduce and dehumanize the individual, we must begin to consider the collective. The degradation of the public space is a profound and threatening problem in our society.

As I have stated before, the individual is only a euphemism, an attractive and artificial designation—the false definition necessary to facilitate the reasoning that illuminates the truth. Even were we to adopt the most individualistic of philosophies, were we to define justice in terms of the maximizing of autonomy, in the Millian sense of absolute autonomy up to the point of restriction of autonomy of the other, we would still have to recognize that the destruction of the public space may ultimately restrict *individual* freedom, as much as other areas which seem to pertain more directly and dramatically to autonomous rights.

Similarly, when we disenfranchise a group of our population, when we deprive them of whatever those resources are that build dignity and compassion, we are of course destroying ourselves. The unity of man is no romantic myth. It is a biological fact that we ignore with peril. Erik Erikson comments:

> . . . As an animal, man is nothing. It is meaningless to speak of a human child as if it were an animal in the process of domestication; or of his instincts as set patterns encroached upon or molded by the autocratic environment. Man's "inborn instincts" are drive-fragments to be assembled, given meaning and organized during a prolonged childhood by methods of child training and schooling which vary from culture to culture and are determined by tradition. In this lies his chance as an organism, as a member of a society, as an individual. In this also lies his limitation. For while the animal survives where his segment of nature remains predictable enough to fit his inborn patterns of instinctive response, or where these responses contain the elements for necessary mutation, man survives only where traditional child training provides him with a conscience which will guide him without crushing him and which is firm and flexible enough to fit the vicissitudes of his historical era.

To talk of the nature of things, of course, is not to talk of the rightness of them. Biologists have been accused of being "natural law" philosophers in the most simplistic sense of that term. I remember well the first time I was so accused. At that point I was not aware of even having a philosophy, and was unsure what natural law meant, let alone what was wrong with it. Six years later, after a baptism in philosophy of sorts (not total immersion), I am still not completely sure what it is nor completely convinced that there is anything wrong with it. At any rate, in terms of the original accusation, I was guilty as charged. There is a tendency, when emerging from the tradition of biology and medicine, to define the "good" in terms of the "normal." It is "normal" to have a blood pressure within a certain range, therefore it is healthy—a medical term for "good"—to have such a blood pressure. We normally have ten fingers and ten toes; therefore, we "ought" to have twenty digits. We are distressed about missing digits; it is not good to have fewer than the normal number, nor for that matter do we honor supernumerary digits. More is no better than less; if it is normal, it is good.

In examining the nature of man in any area, we must remove ourselves from the medical model and eschew the simplistic equation. Of course, even within the medical model we do tend to transgress; it is normal for man to have dental caries, but it is not defined as healthy or good. This tends, however, to be viewed by the typical physician as an intrusion from without, like the infection of the spirochete. In this sense the biologist may be akin to the old-fashioned God-Devil theologian. The normal, healthy body is the gift of God, our endowment, our nature, and the definition of good; disease is an alien and nasty visitation—the domain of the Devil. Still, therefore, we cling to a normal-normative bind.

In discussing the caring nature of man, I hope that what I am saying is that the caring nature of *Homo sapiens* is good, not because it is normal but because it is necessary for the survival of the species and because I visualize goodness as being the burden of that specific species. Perhaps what I am saying then is closer to the "Agere sequitur esse" —the ought *is founded* in the is.

But what is the *esse* in human nature? Part of the wonder of that nature is that what we are is in great part up to us. In a medieval Talmudic text, the question was raised: "If God had intended man to be circumcised, why would he have not created him in such form?" And the answer that was given had a wisdom that transcends the specificity of the question: "Man, alone amongst animals, is created incomplete but with the capacity to complete himself." We are the executors of our future. Our current sense of self is the God in whose image future man will be created.

Recently, political scientists have begun to link the findings of ethology and studies of the genetic, sociological, and psychological aspects of human nature with the discipline of political science. Politics is beginning to be seen as a biological phenomenon. But innate biology alone cannot guide us. Certain reflexive and instinctive behavior no longer serves the same purposes for which it was designed in a pre-cultural time. For example, the larger man must have always been threatening to a smaller man in a primitive setting. Today it depends on who works for whom; most of us have learned not to equate size with power.

Our intuitive and instinctive responses were shaped genetically to a set of pre-cultural conditioning which no longer exists. We have changed the rules of life, redefined the signals of danger and survival, without having changed the in-built reflex response. Our in-built emotions give us dangerously wrong signals for the civilized world we occupy, and we are obliged to reeducate our intuition.

We must redesign ourselves. But we must exercise care that new institutions will not diminish the most human of qualities, or extinguish them in the adult organism. There will be new pressures from a number of sources to disengage the child from his parent; the woman's movement, struggling to free women from the indignity of a gender stereotype that has placed them in a constant state of dependency, must not view this argument about the crucial bind of parent and child as a deterrent to its aspirations. Women must continue to struggle for the right to pride and the right to accomplishment of which they have been deprived for so long. I am not here espousing a "man-hunter, woman-domestic" view of nature. I am only arguing for self-pride. And I am stating the unavoidable fact that all achievement and all pride, all confidence, rests on certain inviolable loving contacts early in life. If a woman then wants to have a child, she should be free to have one without the impediment of sacrificing other creative drives and needs. How this is to be done, I do not know. Certainly it should not be difficult to change our social institutions so that the demands of early childhood will not obstruct or handicap a woman's professional life. Perhaps, as some women have suggested, the primary caring role can be adopted by men. If so, the problem remains the same, except translated to another gender: how to permit a withdrawal from professional life to devote the time to this urgent requirement of all life and still allow for a reentry without penalty. If we are to attempt to switch the primary caring agent, then even more urgency is added to the requirement that we fully understand the components of this interrelationship. The solution is not to deny its importance.

Similarly, the pressure for public day care centers will create new problems. Jacob Gewirtz in his studies of child-rearing in Israel demonstrated the kind of meticulous study that is necessary in these vital areas. Using the advantage of the variable methods of child-rearing in Israel, he compared four groups of children: those raised in institutions, those raised in day care centers, those raised in communal kibbutzim, and those raised in urban families. He used the simple variable of smiling as his measurement. As early as ten months one can notice a difference, with a significantly greater amount of smiling in the family-raised child from the other three, and this difference becomes progressively greater with time. We know the destructiveness of bad institutions. What Gewirtz demonstrated was that even better institutions, even "non-institutional" institutions, seem to diminish (at least by the measure of one reasonable variable) attributes that are basic to the concept of childhood we desire. The family may not be inviolate, but we attack it at our peril; if we are to move away from it, we had best do so slowly, with tested alternatives and a recognizable accounting of the prices we are likely to pay. I suspect it is an indispensable necessity for the kinds of human beings I am willing to call human. Therefore, we had best think in terms of optional modifications rather than abolition.

There are other concerns about early child care centers. They are bringing the young out of the structure of the family at an even earlier age, which will lead to even more of the homogenization discussed above, and therefore even further reduce the security that variability produces. It is also inconceivable that any group of educators could bring together large groups of children for large amounts of time and merely "care" for them without trying to improve (educate) them.

Experimentation, unconscious or otherwise, within a family has the safety of small numbers. Experimentation with larger and larger groups runs great risk of selectively breeding out that which is treasured and only enters consciousness with its absence. We have seen this happen time and time again. To take a crude and simple example, for years the rose hybridizers focused on developing precisely the kind of rose most treasured by gardeners: high-centered, brilliantly colored, single-stemmed, disease-resistant, shiny-foliaged, fully double roses were developed which, only after the fact, were discovered to have lost that essential ingredient, their scent, that by any name made them identifiable as a rose. There is much in the sweetness of human nature which is vulnerable to change; there is much that is already changed. We must respect the goodness in ourselves; to do so, we must continue to acknowledge its presence.

The caring nature of human beings is so self-evident as to escape our observation if we are not careful. It has survived many periods of self-doubt and self-abuse. We are now in such a time. And here perhaps another last look at clinical depression may allow for some vision of hope, for some vestige of the pathway even through despair.

The depressive patient has given up all hope of either fight or flight, but these are not the only survival mechanisms. They are not even the most fundamental. *Dependency* is the basic survival mechanism of the human organism. In the critical early period of life, the human animal is capable of neither fight nor flight—only clutch and cling. In the human being, with his disproportionately long period of helplessness, the very survival of the species is based on the built-in dependency maneuvers of the infant and the biologically determined sympathetic responses they elicit in the adult.

When the adult gives up hope in his ability to cope and sees himself incapable of either fleeing or fighting, he is "reduced" to a state of depression. This very reduction, with its parallel to the helplessness of infancy, becomes, ironically, one last unconscious cry for help—a plea for a solution to the problem of survival via dependency, a call for love. The very stripping of one's defenses becomes a form of defensive maneuver. It is part of the wonder of the human being that even the state of hopelessness can be used to generate hope. We must hope, as Shelley said, "till hope creates from its own wreck the thing it contemplates."

Our greatest hope is in our nature. It is good—if not all good. But it is of our nature to change our nature. We are always in the process of designing our descendants; I am here suggesting that there must be limits set to what can be changed, since certain fundamentals of our nature, such as caring, are essential for survival. With technology we may fly without wings, exist under the oceans, survive our own hearts and lungs and whatever other technological advances the future holds—as unthinkable to us today, and as inevitable as the ones I just listed were to a human being of only one hundred years ago. But there will be one sure limit on where that technology can take us. If we bend our nature too far, if we allow that technology, like the horns of the elk, to lead to an evolution too far from our basic needs and pursuits, we will be destroyed. We must, above all, respect the forces that bind us to others with love and concern, for that ensures the survival of a social matrix on whose existence we as a species depend for life.

Caring and loving we are, and caring and loving we must be—caring and loving we *will be* as long as we so perceive ourselves. In other ways we are free to change, modify, adapt, and move. We are changing the rules of existence. We *should* change the rules of existence. We have a right to do so, and in certain cases, even a need to do so. Our natures will evolve in yet unanticipated ways, and that is as it should be. But to caring we must cling.

BIBLIOGRAPHY

Abraham, K. "Psychoanalytic Studies on Character Formation," in *Selected Papers on Psychoanalysis*. London: Hogarth Press, 1949, Chs. 23, 24, 25, pp. 370–418.

————. "Notes on the Psycho-Analytical Investigation and Treatment of Manic-Depressive Insanity and Allied Conditions," 1911, in *Selected Papers*. London: Hogarth Press, 1927.

Ainsworth, M. D. S. "Attachment and Dependency: A Review," in J. L. Gerwirtz (ed.), *Attachment and Dependency*. Washington, D.C.: V. H. Winston & Sons, 1972.

————. "The Development of Infant-Mother Attachment," in B. M. Caldwell and H. N. Ricciuti (eds.), *Review of Child Development Research*. Vol. III. Chicago: University of Chicago Press, 1973.

————. "The Development of Infant-Mother Interaction Among the Ganda," in B. M. Foss (ed.), *Determinants of Infant Behavior*. Vol. II. London: Methuen; New York: John Wiley, 1963.

————. "The Effects of Maternal Deprivation: A Review of Findings and Controversy, Privation of Maternal Care: A Reassessment of Its Effects." Geneva: WHO Public Health Paper No. 14: 97–165, 1962.

————. *Infancy in Uganda: Infant Care and the Growth of Love*. Baltimore: Johns Hopkins University Press, 1967.

————. "Object Relations, Dependency and Attachment: A Theoretical Review of the Infant-Mother Relationship," *Child Development*, 1969, 40, 969–1025.

Ainsworth, M. D. S., and Wittig, B. A. "Attachment and Exploratory Behavior of One-Year-Olds in a Strange Situation," in B. M. Foss (ed.), *Determinants of Infant Behavior*. Vol. IV. London: Methuen; New York: John Wiley, 1969.

Alexander, F. "Treatment of a Case of Peptic Ulcer and Personality Disorder," *Psychosomatic Medicine*, 1947, 9, 320.

Ambrose, A. (ed.). *Stimulation in Early Infancy*. London & New York: Academic Press, 1969.

Ardrey, Robert. *African Genesis*. New York: Atheneum, 1961.

————. *The Territorial Imperative*. New York: Atheneum, 1966.

Axelrad, S., and Maury, L. M. "Identification as a Mechanism of Adaptation," in G. B. Wilbur and W. Meunsterburger (eds.), *Psychoanalysis and Culture.* New York: International Universities Press, 1951, pp. 168–84.

Balint, A. "Identification," *International Journal of Psychoanalysis*, 1943, 24, 97–107.

Barlow, H., and Pettigrew, J. "Lack of Specificity of Neurones in the Visual Cortex of Young Kittens," *Journal of Physiology*, 1971, 218, 98–100.

Barnett, D., Leiderman, P. H., Grobstein, R., and Klaus, M. H. "Neonatal Separation: The Maternal Side of Interactional Deprivation," *Pediatrics*, 1970, 45, 197–205.

Barrett, W. *Irrational Man.* Garden City, N.Y.: Anchor Books, Doubleday, 1962.

Bell, S. M. "The Development of the Concept of Object as Related to Infant-Mother Attachment," *Child Development*, 1970, 41, 291–311.

Benedek, T. "Adaptation to Reality in Early Infancy," *Psychoanalytic Quarterly*, 1938, 7, 200–15.

———. "The Psychosomatic Implications of the Primary Unit: Mother-Child," *American Journal of Orthopsychiatry*, 1949, 19, 642–54.

Benjamin, J. D. "Some Developmental Observations Relating to the Theory of Anxiety," *Journal of the American Psychoanalytic Association*, 1961, 9, 652–68.

Beres, D. "Superego and Depression," in R. M. Lowenstein, L. M. Newman, M. Schue, and A. J. Solnit (eds.), *Psychoanalysis—A General Psychology.* New York: International Universities Press, 1968, pp. 479–98.

———. "Vicissitudes of Superego Functions and Superego Precursors in Childhood," *The Psychoanalytic Study of the Child*, 1958, 13, 324–35.

———. "The Humaneness of Human Beings: Psychoanalytic Considerations," *Psychoanalytic Quarterly*, 1968, 37, 487–522.

Bettelheim, B. "Personality Formation in the Kibbutz," *American Journal of Psychoanalysis*, 1969, 29(1), 3–9.

———. *The Empty Fortress: Infantile Autism and the Birth of the Self.* New York: The Free Press, 1967.

Bibring, E. "The Mechanisms of Depression," in P. Greenacre (ed.), *Affective Disorders.* New York: International Universities Press, 1953.

Bieber, I. *Homosexuality: A Psychoanalytic Study.* New York: Basic Books, 1962.

Bowlby, J. *Attachment and Loss.* Vol. 1. *Attachment.* New York: Basic Books, 1969.

———. *Attachment and Loss.* Vol. 2. *Separation: Anxiety and Anger.* New York: Basic Books, 1973.

———. "The Nature of a Child's Tie to Its Mother," *International Journal of Psychoanalysis*, 1958, 39, 350–73.

Brazelton, T. B., School, M. L., and Robey, J. S. "Visual Responses in the Newborn," *Pediatrics*, 1966, 37, 284–90.

———, Koslowski, B., and Main, M., in M. Lewis and L. Rosenblum (eds.),

The Effect of the Infant on Its Caregiver. New York: John Wiley, pp. 49–76.

Bretall, R. *A Kierkegaard Anthology.* New York: Modern Library, 1963.

Brody, S. *Patterns of Mothering.* New York: International Universities Press, 1956.

Bruch, H. "Psychiatric Aspects of Obesity," *Metabolism,* 6, 461–5, 1957.

Buber, M. *The Knowledge of Man.* London: Allen & Unwin, 1965, pp. 123–4.

Burlingham, D., and Freud, A. *Infants Without Families.* London: Allen & Unwin, 1944.

Cairns, R. B. "Attachment and Dependency: A Psychobiological and Social-Learning Synthesis," in Gewirtz (ed.), *Attachment and Dependency, op. cit.,* pp. 29–80.

Chodoff, P., and Lyons, H. "Hysteria, the Hysterical Personality and 'Hysterical' Conversion," *American Journal of Psychiatry,* 1958, 114, 734–40.

Cohen, L. J. "The Operational Definition of Human Attachment," *Psychological Bulletin,* 1974, 81, 207–14.

D'Arcy, M. C. *The Mind and Heart of Love.* New York: Meridian Books, 1956.

DeRougemont, Denis. *Love in the Western World.* New York: Pantheon Books, 1956.

De Saussure, R. "Identification and Substitution," *International Journal of Psychoanalysis,* 1939, 20, 465–70.

Dobzhansky, Theodosius. *Evolution, Genetics, and Man.* New York: John Wiley, 1955.

———. *Mankind Evolving.* New Haven, Conn.: Yale University Press, 1962.

Dubos, René. *Man Adapting.* New Haven, Conn.: Yale University Press, 1965.

———. *So Human an Animal.* New York: Charles Scribner's Sons, 1968.

Easser, B. R. and Lesser, S. R. "Hysterical Personality: A Re-evaluation," *Psychoanalytic Quarterly,* 1965, 34, 390–405.

Eininger, M., and Hill, J. P. "Instrumental and Affectional Dependency and Nurturance in Preschool Children," *Journal of Genetic Psychology,* 1969, 115, 277–84.

Elkisch, P. "The Psychological Significance of the Mirror," *Journal of the American Psychoanalytic Association,* 1957, 5, 235–44.

Erikson, E. H. *Childhood and Society.* 2nd edition, New York: Norton, 1963.

———. *Identity and the Life Cycle.* New York: International Universities Press, 1959.

———. *Identity: Youth and Crisis.* New York: Norton, 1968.

Fenichel, O. "Identification," *The Collected Papers of Otto Fenichel.* Vol. I. New York: Norton, 1953, pp. 97–113.

———. *The Psychoanalytic Theory of Neurosis.* New York: Norton, 1945, pp. 129–40, 463–540.

Foss, B. M. (ed.). *Determinants of Infant Behavior*. Vols. I–IV. London: Methuen; New York: John Wiley, 1961–69.

Fraiberg, S. "Libidinal Object Constancy and Mental Representation," *The Psychoanalytic Study of the Child*, 1969, 24, 9–47.

———. "Separation Crisis in Two Blind Children," *The Psychoanalytic Study of the Child*, 1971, 26, 355–71.

Freud, A. "Psychoanalysis and Education," *The Psychoanalytic Study of the Child*, 1954, 9, 9–15.

———. "Discussion of Dr. John Bowlby's Paper," *The Psychoanalytic Study of the Child*, 1960, 15, 53–63.

———. "The Ego and the Mechanisms of Defense," *The Writings of Anna Freud*. Vol. II. New York: International Universities Press, 1936.

——— and Dann, S. "An Experiment in Group Upbringing," *The Psychoanalytic Study of the Child*, 1951, 6, 127–68.

Freud, S. *Beyond the Pleasure Principle*, 1920. Standard Edition, Vol. XVIII. London: Hogarth Press, 1955.

———. "Character and Anal Erotism," *Collected Papers*, Vol. XI, p. 45; Standard Edition, Vol. IX. London: Hogarth Press, 1966, p. 167.

———. *Civilization and Its Discontents*, 1930. Standard Edition, Vol. XXI.

———. *Economic Problems in Masochism*, 1924.

———. "Female Sexuality," 1931. Standard Edition, Vol. XXI. London: Hogarth Press, 1961.

———. "Fragment of an Analysis of a Case of Hysteria [Dora]," 1905. Standard Edition, Vol. VII. London: Hogarth Press, 1953.

———. *Group Psychology and the Analysis of the Ego*, 1921. Standard Edition, Vol. XVIII. London: Hogarth Press, 1955.

———. "Inhibitions, Symptoms and Anxiety," 1926, Standard Edition, Vol. XX. London: Hogarth Press, 1959.

———. *The Interpretation of Dreams*, 1900. Standard Edition, Vols. IV, V. London: Hogarth Press, 1966.

———. *Mourning and Melancholia*, 1917. Standard Edition, Vol. XIV. London: Hogarth Press, 1957.

———. "Notes upon a Case of Obsessional Neurosis [the "Rat Man"]," 1909. Standard Edition, Vol. X. London: Hogarth Press, 1955.

———. *Obsessive Action and Religious Practices*, 1907. Standard Edition, Vol. IX.

———. *An Outline of Psychoanalysis*. Standard Edition, Vol. XXIII. London: Hogarth Press, 1938.

———. "The Predisposition to Obsessional Neurosis," 1913. Standard Edition, Vol. XII. London: Hogarth Press, 1958, pp. 311–26.

———. *Totem and Taboo*, 1912. Standard Edition, Vol. XIII.

Fromm, Erich. *The Art of Loving*. New York: Bantam Books, Harper & Row, 1956, p. 33.

Fromm-Reichmann, F. "On Loneliness," in D. M. Bullard (ed.), *Selected Papers of Frieda Fromm-Reichmann*. Chicago: The University of Chicago Press, 1959, pp. 325–36.

Fuchs, S. E. "On Introjection," *International Journal of Psychoanalysis,* 1937, 18, 269–93.

Furer, M. "The History of the Superego Concept in Psychoanalysis: A Review of the Literature," in S. C. Post (ed.), *Moral Values and Superego Concept in Psychoanalysis.* New York: International Universities Press, 1972, pp. 11–63.

Gergen, K. J. *The Concept of Self.* New York: Holt, Rinehart & Winston, 1971.

Gewirtz, J. L. (ed.). *Attachment and Dependency.* Washington, D.C.: V. H. Winston & Sons, 1972.

———. "A Learning Analysis of the Effects of Normal Stimulation, Privation and Deprivation on the Acquisition of Social Motivation and Attachment," in Foss (ed.), *Determinants of Infant Behavior,* Vol. I, pp. 213–99.

———. "The Course of Infant Smiling in Four Child-Rearing Environments in Israel," in Foss (ed.), *Determinants of Infant Behavior,* Vol. III, pp. 205–48.

———. "Mechanisms of Social Learning: Some Roles of Stimulation and Behavior in Early Human Development," in D. A. Geslin (ed.), *Handbook of Socialization Theory and Research.* Chicago: Rand McNally, 1969, pp. 52–212.

Gewirtz, J. L., and Stingle, K. G. "Learning in Generalized Imitation as the Basis of Identification," *Psychological Review,* 1968, 75, 374–97.

Glover, E. "The Neurotic Character," in *On the Early Development of the Mind.* New York: International Universities Press, pp. 47–66.

Goffman, E. *The Presentation of Self in Everyday Life.* Garden City, N.Y.: Anchor Books, Doubleday, 1959.

Goldfarb, W. "Psychological Privation in Infancy and Subsequent Adjustment," *American Journal of Orthopsychiatry,* 1945, 15, 247–55.

Gouin Decarie, T. *Intelligence and Affectivity in Early Childhood.* New York: International Universities Press, 1965.

Gould, R. *Child Studies Through Fantasy: Cognitive-Affective Patterns in Development.* New York: Quadrangle Books, 1972.

Greenacre, P. "Physical Determinants in the Development of the Sense of Identity," *Journal of the American Psychoanalytic Association,* 1958, 6, 612–27.

——— (ed.). *Affective Disorders.* New York: International Universities Press, 1953.

Greenson, R. R. "The Struggle Against Identification," *Journal of the American Psychoanalytic Association,* 1934, 2, 200–17.

Griffin, G. A., and Harlow, H. F. "Effects of Three Months of Total Social Deprivation on Social Adjustment and Learning in the Rhesus Monkey," *Child Development,* 1966, 37, 533–47.

Hamburg, D. A. "Observations of Mother-Infant Interactions in Primate Field Studies," in Foss (ed.), *Determinants of Infant Behavior,* Vol. IV, pp. 3–14.

Harlow, H. F. "The Nature of Love," *American Psychologist*, 1958, 13, 673–85.

——. "The Development of Affectional Patterns in Infant Monkeys," Foss (ed.), *Determinants of Infant Behavior*, Vol. I, pp. 75–97.

——. "The Maternal Affectional System," in *Maternal Behavior in Mammals*, H. L. Rheingold (ed.), New York: John Wiley, 1963.

—— and Zimmermann, R. R. "Affectional Responses in the Infant Monkey," *Science*, 1959, 130, 421.

—— and Harlow, M. K. "The Affectional Systems," in A. M. Schrier, H. F. Harlow, and F. Stollnitz (eds.), *Behavior of Nonhuman Primates*. Vol. II. New York & London: New York: Academic Press, 1965.

—— and Harlow, M. K. "Effects of Various Mother-Infant Relationships on Rhesus Monkey Behaviors," in Foss (ed.), *Determinants of Infant Behavior*, Vol. IV, pp. 15–36.

——, Harlow, M. K., and Hansen, E. W. "The Maternal Affectional System of Rhesus Monkeys," in H. L. Rheingold (ed.), *Maternal Behavior in Mammals*. New York: John Wiley, 1963, pp. 254–81.

——. "Love in Infant Monkeys," *Scientific American*, 1959, 200, 68–74.

Hatfield, J. S., Ferguson, L. R., and Alpert, R. "Mother-Child Interaction and the Socialization Process," *Child Development*, 1967, 38, 365–414.

Heidegger, M. *Being and Time*. New York: Harper & Row, 1962.

Heinicke, C., and Westheimer, I. *Brief Separations*. New York: International Universities Press, 1966.

Hendrik, I. "Early Development of the Ego: Identification in Infancy," *Psychoanalytic Quarterly*, 1951, 20, 44–61.

Hersher, L., Richmond, J. B., and Moore, A. V. "Modifiability of the Critical Period for the Development of Maternal Behavior in Sheep and Goats," *Behavior*, 1963, 20, 311–20.

Huxley, Julian. *Man in the Modern World*. New York: Mentor Books (The New American Library), 1944.

Jacobson, E. "Contribution of the Metapsychology of Psychotic Identification," *Journal of the American Psychoanalytic Association*, 1954, 2, 239–62.

——. *The Self and the Object World*. New York: International Universities Press, 1964.

——. "The Self and the Object World," *The Psychoanalytic Study of the Child*, 1954, 9, 75–127.

Johnson, A., and Szurek, S. "The Genesis of Antisocial Acting Out in Children and Adults," *Psychoanalytic Quarterly*, 1952, 21, 323–43.

Kagan, J. "Acquisition and Significance of Sex-Typing and Sex-Role Identity," in M. Hoffman and L. W. Hoffman (eds.), *Review of Child Development*. Vol. I. New York: Russell Sage, 1964, 137–67.

——. "The Concept of Identification," *Psychological Review*, 1958, 65, 296–305.

Kapp, F., Rosenbaum, M., and Romano, J. "Psychological Factors in Men with Peptic Ulcers," *American Journal of Psychiatry*, 1947, 103, 700.

Kennell, John, Trause, Mary Anne, and Klaus, Marshall. "Evidence for a

Sensitive Period in the Human Mother." To be published by Ciba Books.

Kennell, John, Trause, Mary Anne, and Klaus, Marshall. "Does Human Maternal Behavior after Delivery Show a Characteristic Pattern?" To be published by Ciba Books.

Klaus, M. D., Kennell, J. H., Plumb, N., and Zuehlke, S. "Maternal Behavior at the First Contact with Her Young," *Pediatrics*, 1970, 46, 187–92.

Klein, M. "On Identification." In M. Klein, P. Heinmann, and R. E. Money-Kyrtle (eds.), *New Directions in Psychoanalysis*. New York: Basic Books, 1955, pp. 309–45.

Klopfer, P. H., Adams, D. K., and Klopfer, M. S. "Maternal 'Imprinting' in Goats," *Proceedings of the National Academy of Sciences*, 1964, 52, 911.

———. "Mother Love: What Turns It On?" *American Science*, 1971, 59, 404–7.

Knight, R. P. "Introjection, Projection and Identification," *Psychoanalytic Quarterly*, 1940, 9, 334–41.

Koff, R. H. "A Definition of Identification: A Review of the Literature," *International Journal of Psychoanalysis*, 1961, 42, 362–70.

Kohlberg, L. "Moral Development and Identification," *National Society for the Study of Education Yearbook*, 1963, 62, Part I, 277–332.

Laing, R. D. *Self and Others*. Harmondsworth, Middlesex: Pelican Books, 1971.

Levy, D. "Developmental and Psychodynamic Aspects of Oppositional Behavior," in S. Rado and G. E. Daniels (eds.), *Changing Concepts of Psychoanalytic Medicine*. New York: Grune & Stratton, 1956, pp. 114–34.

Lichtenstein, H. "The Dilemma of Human Identity; Notes on Self Transformation, Self Observation and Metamorphosis," *Journal of the American Psychoanalytic Association*, 1963, 2, 173–223.

———. "Identity and Sexuality: A Study of Their Interrelationship in Man," *Journal of the American Psychoanalytic Association*, 1964, 9, 179–260.

———. "The Role of Narcissism in the Emergence and Maintenance of a Primary Identity," *International Journal of Psychoanalysis*, 1961, 45, 49–56.

Liebert, R. *Radical and Militant Youth*. New York: Praeger, 1971.

Lipsitt, L. P. "Learning Processes of Human Newborns," *Merrill-Palmer Quarterly*, 1966, 45, 71.

Lorenz, Konrad Z. *On Aggression*. New York: Harcourt, Brace & World, 1966.

———. "The Companion in the Bird's World," *Auk*, 1937, 54, 245–73.

Lustman, S. "Defense, Symptom and Character," *The Psychoanalytic Study of the Child*, 1962, 17, pp. 216–44.

Lynd, H. M. *On Shame and the Search for Identity*. New York: Harcourt, Brace, 1958.

188   Bibliography

Maccoby, E. E., and Masters, J. C. "Attachment and Dependency," in P. H. Mussen (ed.), *Carmichael's Manual of Child Psychology*. 3rd edition. Vol. II. New York: John Wiley, 1970, pp. 73–158.

───── and Feldman, S. S. "Mother-Attachment and Stranger-Reactions in the Third Year," *Monographs of the Society for Research in Child Development*, 1972, 37.

Mahler, M. S. "Autism and Symbiosis: Two Extreme Disturbances of Identity," *International Journal of Psychoanalysis*, 1958, 39, 77–83.

─────. "On the First Three Subphases of the Separation-Individuation Process," *International Journal of Psychoanalysis*, 1972, 53, 333–8.

─────. "On Human Symbiosis and the Vicissitudes of Individuation," *Infantile Psychosis*. Vol. I. New York: International Universities Press, 1968.

─────. "Symbiosis and Individuation—The Psychological Birth of the Human Infant," *The Psychoanalytic Study of the Child*, 1974, 24, 89–106.

Marmor, J. *Sexual Inversion: The Multiple Roots of Homosexuality*. New York: Basic Books, 1965.

Masters, Roger D. "Genes, Language, and Evolution," in *Semiotica*, 1970, Vol. II, No. 4. The Hague: Mouton & Co.

─────. "The Impact of Ethology on Political Science," in *Biology and Politics: Some Recent Explorations*. The Hague: Mouton & Co., 1975.

─────. "Politics as a Biological Phenomenon," in *Social Science Information*, April 1975, The Hague: Mouton & Co.

May, Rollo. *Love and Will*. New York: Norton, 1969.

Mayeroff, M. *On Caring*. New York: Harper & Row, 1971.

Mead, G. H. *Mind, Self and Society*. Chicago: University of Chicago Press, 1934.

Meissner, W. W. "Notes on Identification: I. Origins in Freud," *Psychoanalytic Quarterly*, 1970, 39, 563–89.

─────. "Notes on Identification: II. Clarification of Related Concepts," *Psychoanalytic Quarterly*, 1971, 40, 277–302.

─────. "Notes on Identification: III. The Concept of Identification," *Psychoanalytic Quarterly*, 1972, 41, 224–60.

Michael, J. "Character Structure and Character Disorders," in S. Arieti (ed.), *American Handbook of Psychiatry*. Vol. I. New York: Basic Books, 1959, pp. 353–73.

Michels, R. "Student Dissent," *Journal of the American Psychoanalytic Association*, 1971, 19, 417–32.

Mitchell, G. D., Raymond, E. J., Ruppenthal, G. C., and Harlow, H. F. "Long-term Effects of Total Social Isolation upon Behavior of Rhesus Monkeys," *Psychological Report*, 1966, 18, 567–80.

Modell, A. H. *Object Love and Reality*. New York: International Universities Press, 1968.

Moffett, James. *Love in the New Testament*. London: Hodder & Stoughton, 1929.

Montagu, A. *Touching: The Human Significance of the Skin.* New York: Columbia University Press, 1971.

Moore, T. "Children of Working Mothers," in S. Yudkin and H. Holme (eds.), *Working Mothers and Their Children.* London: Michael Joseph, 1963.

Morgan, G. A., and Ricciuti, H. N. "Infants' Responses to Strangers During the First Year," in Foss (ed.), *Determinants of Infant Behavior,* Vol. IV, pp. 253–272.

Morris, Desmond. *The Naked Ape.* New York, McGraw-Hill, 1956.

Nelson, C. Ellis (ed.). *Conscience, Theological and Psychological Perspectives.* New York: Newman Press, 1973.

Nygren, Anders. *Agape and Eros.* Philadelphia: The Westminster Press, 1953.

Olden, C. "Notes on the Development of Empathy," *The Psychoanalytic Study of the Child,* 1958, 13, 505–18.

———. "On Adult Empathy with Children," *The Psychoanalytic Study of the Child,* 1953, 8, 11–126.

Ovesey, L. *Homosexuality and Pseudohomosexuality.* New York: Aronson, 1969.

Papousek, H., and Bernstein, P. "The Functions of Conditioning Stimulation in Human Neonates and Infants," in A. Ambrose (ed.), *Stimulation in Early Infancy.* New York & London: Academic Press, 1969.

Parsons, T., and Bales, R. F. *Family Socialization and Interaction Process.* New York: The Free Press, 1955.

Payne, D. E., and Mussen, P. H. "Parent-Child Relations and Father Identifications Among Adolescent Boys," *Journal of Abnormal and Social Psychology,* 1958, 52, 358–62.

Piaget, J. *The Construction of Reality in the Child.* New York: Basic Books, 1954.

———. *Play, Dreams and Imitation in Childhood.* New York: Norton, 1962.

———. *The Psychology of Intelligence.* Totowa, N.J.: Littlefield, Adams & Co., 1966.

Portmann, Adolf. *Animals as Social Beings.* New York: Harper & Row, 1964.

Post, Seymour C. *Moral Values and the Superego Concept in Psychoanalysis.* New York: International Universities Press, 1972.

Pynchon, T. *Gravity's Rainbow.* New York: Viking Press, 1973.

Rado, S. "Psychodynamics of Depression from the Etiologic Point of View," *Psychosomatic Medicine,* Vol. 13, No. 1 (Jan.–Feb. 1951), 51–5.

———. *Psychoanalysis of Behavior: Collected Papers.* New York: Grune & Stratton, 1956.

———. "The Problem of Melancholia," *International Journal of Psychoanalysis,* 1928, 9, 420.

Rawls, J. *Theory of Justice.* Cambridge: Harvard University Press, 1971.

Reich, A. "Early Identifications as Archaic Elements in the Superego," *Journal of the American Psychoanalytic Association,* 1954, 2, 218–38.

Reich, W. *Character Analysis.* New York: Orgone Institute Press, 1949, Parts I & II.

Rheingold, H. L. "The Effect of a Strange Environment on the Behavior of Infants," in Foss (ed), *Determinants of Infant Behavior,* Vol. IV, pp. 137–166.

Rheingold, H. (ed.). *Maternal Behavior in Animals.* New York: John Wiley, 1963.

Rheingold, H. L., and Eckerman, C. O. "Fear of the Stranger: A Critical Examination," in H. W. Reese (ed.), *Advances in Child Development and Behavior.* New York and London: Academic Press, 1973.

Ritvo, S. "The Relationship of Early Ego Identifications to Superego Formation," *International Journal of Psychoanalysis,* 1960, 41, 295–300.

———— and Solnit, A. J. "Influences of Early Mother-Child Interaction on Identification Processes," *The Psychoanalytic Study of the Child,* 1958, 13, 64–85.

Robertson, J., and Robertson, J. "Young Children in Brief Separations: A Fresh Look," *The Psychoanalytic Study of the Child,* 1971, 26, 264–315.

Rosenthal, M. K. "The Generalization of Dependency Behavior from Mother to Stranger," *Journal of Child Psychology and Psychiatry,* 1967, 8, 117–33.

————. "The Effect of a Novel Situation and Anxiety on Two Groups of Dependency Behavior," *British Journal of Psychology,* 1967, 58, 357–64.

Roth, L. I., and Rosenblatt, J. S. "Mammary Glands of Pregnant Rats: Development Stimulated by Licking," *Science,* 1965, 151, 1403–4.

Sandler, J. "On the Concept of the Superego," *The Psychoanalytic Study of the Child,* 1960, 15, 128–62.

———— and Rosenblatt, B. "The Concept of the Representational World," *The Psychoanalytic Study of the Child,* 1962, 17, 139–58.

Sanford, N. "The Dynamics of Identification," *Psychological Review,* 1955, 62, 106–18.

Schafer, R. *Aspects of Internalization.* New York: International Universities Press, 1968.

————. "Psychoanalysis without Psychodynamics," *International Journal of Psychoanalysis,* 1975, 56, 41.

Schaffer, H. R. "Objective Observations of Personality Development in Early Infancy," *British Journal of Medical Psychology,* 1958, 31, 174–83.

————. "Some Issues for Research in the Study of Attachment Behavior," in Foss (ed.), *Determinants of Infant Behavior,* Vol. II, pp. 179–96.

———— and Emerson, P. E. "The Development of Social Attachments in Infancy," *Monographs of the Society for Research in Child Development,* 1964, 23, 1–77.

———— and Emerson, P. E. "Patterns of Response to Physical Contact in Early Human Development," *Journal of Child Psychology and Psychiatry,* 1964, 5, 1–13.

Schur, M. "Discussion of Dr. John Bowlby's Paper," *The Psychoanalytic Study of the Child*, 1960, 15, 63–85.

Sears, R. "Attachment, Dependency and Frustration," in Gewirtz (ed.), *Attachment and Dependency, op. cit.*, pp. 1–27.

Seay, B., Hansen, E., and Harlow, H. F. "Mother-Infant Separation in Monkeys," *Journal of Child Psychology and Psychiatry*, 1962, 3, 123–32.

Simpson, George Gaylord. *The Meaning of Evolution*. New York: Mentor Books (The New American Library), 1950.

Singer, Irving. *The Nature of Love*. New York: Random House, 1966.

Singer, Peter. *Animal Liberation*. New York: Random House, 1976.

Spelke, E., Zelazo, P., Kagan, J., and Kotelchuck, M. "Father Interaction and Separation Protest," *Developmental Psychology*, 1973, 9, 83–90.

Spencer-Booth, Y., and Hinde, R. A. "The Effects of Separating Rhesus Monkey Infants from Their Mothers for Six Days," *Journal of Child Psychology and Psychiatry*, 1966, 7, 179–97.

Spitz, R. A. "Discussion of Dr. John Bowlby's Paper." *The Psychoanalytic Study of the Child*, 1960, 15, 85–95.

———. "Hospitalization: An Inquiry into the Genesis of Psychiatric Conditions in Early Childhood," *The Psychoanalytic Study of the Child*, 1945, 1, 53–74.

———. *The First Year of Life*. New York: International Universities Press, 1965.

———. "Anxiety in Infancy: A Study of Its Manifestations in the First Year of Life," *International Journal of Psychoanalysis*, 1950, 31, 138–43.

———. "Unhappy and Fatal Outcomes of Emotional Deprivation and Stress in Infancy," In I. Galdston (ed.), *Beyond the Germ Theory*. New York: Health Education Council, 1954, pp. 120–31.

Stayton, D. J., and Ainsworth, M. D. S. "Individual Differences in Infant Responses to Brief Everyday Separations as Related to Other Infant and Maternal Behaviors," *Developmental Psychology*, 1973, 9, 226–35.

Stayton, D. J., Ainsworth, M. D. S., and Main, M. E. "Development of Separation Behavior in the First Year of Life: Protest, Following and Greeting," *Developmental Psychology*, 1973, 9, 213–25.

Stone, C. D. *Should Trees Have Standing?*, Los Altos, Calif.: William Kaufman, Inc., 1974.

Sullivan, H. S. *Clinical Studies in Psychiatry*. New York: Norton, 1956.

———. *The Interpersonal Theory of Psychiatry*. New York: Norton, 1953.

Szasz, T. "Factors in the Psychogenesis of Peptic Ulcer," *Psychosomatic Medicine*, 1949, 11, 300.

Tax, S. *Evolution After Darwin*. Vol. III, pp. 273–82, as quoted in Dobzhansky, *Mankind Evolving*, 1962, p. 22.

Taylor, J. L. *The Stages of Human Life*, 1921, p. 157, as quoted in Montagu, *op. cit.*

Tennes, K., and Lampl, E. "Stranger and Separation Anxiety in Infancy," *Journal of Nervous and Mental Disorders*, 1964, 139, 247–54.

———. "Some Aspects of the Mother-Child Relationship Pertaining to

Infantile Separation Anxiety," *Journal of Nervous and Mental Disorders*, 1966, 143, 426–37.

Thorson, Thomas Landon. *Biopolitics*. New York: Holt, Rinehart & Winston, 1970.

Tiger, Lionel, and Fox, Robin. *The Imperial Animal*. New York: Holt, Rinehart & Winston, 1971.

Tomkins, S. *Affect, Imagery, Consciousness*. Vol. I. New York: Springer, 1962.

Twain, M. (Clemens, S.) *Adventures of Huckleberry Finn*. New York: Harper & Row, 1896.

Valenstein, A. F. "The Earliest Mother-Child Relationship and the Development of the Superego," in Post (ed.), *Moral Values and the Superego Concept in Psychoanalysis, op. cit.*, pp. 63–74.

Wheelis, A. *The Quest for Identity*. New York: Norton, 1958.

White, R. W. "Ego and Reality in Psychoanalytic Theory," *Psychological Issues*, 1964, 3, Monograph 11.

———. "Competence and the Psychosexual Stages of Development," in M. R. Jones (ed.), *Nebraska Symposium on Motivation*. Lincoln, Neb.: University of Nebraska Press, 1960.

———. "Motivation Reconsidered: A Concept of Competence," *Psychological Review*, 1959, 66, 297–333.

Wiesel, T., and Hubel, D. "Single Cell Responses in Striate Cortex of Kittens Deprived of Vision in One Eye," *Journal of Neurophysiology*, 1963, 26, 1003–17.

Williams, D. D. *The Spirit and the Forms of Love*. New York: Harper & Row, 1968.

Winestine, M. C. "The Experience of Separation-Individuation and Its Reverberations Through the Course of Life. I: Infancy and Childhood," *Journal of the American Psychoanalytic Association*, 1973, 21, 135–54.

Winnicott, D. W. "Transitional Objects and Transitional Phenomena," *International Journal of Psychoanalysis*, 1953, 34, 1–9.

———. "The Capacity to Be Alone," *International Journal of Psychoanalysis*, 1958, 39, 416–20.

———. "The Theory of the Parent-Infant Relationship," *International Journal of Psychoanalysis*, 1960, 41, 585–95.

Wolff, P. H. "Observations on the Early Developments of Smiling," in Foss (ed.), *Determinants of Infant Behavior, op. cit.*, Vol. II, pp. 113–34.

Yarrow, L. J. "Attachment and Dependency: A Developmental Perspective," in Gewirtz (ed.), *Attachment and Dependency, op. cit.*, pp. 81–95.

———. "Separation From Parents During Early Childhood," *Review of Child Development Research*, 1964, 1, 89–136.

NOTES

Chapter I

Page	Line	
7	9	W. Barrett, 1962.
10	7	For discussions of the "hostile, territorial, aggressive aspects of human behavior," see Konrad Lorenz, 1966; Robert Ardrey, 1966; Desmond Morris, 1967; and Lionel Tiger, 1971.
11	1	John Gardner, *The Wreckage of Agathon*. New York: Harper & Row, 1970, p. 11.
11	32	T. H. White, *The Once and Future King*. New York: G. P. Putnam's Sons, 1958, p. 195.

Chapter II

15	11	Julian Huxley, *Man in the Modern World*, pp. 16–17.
17	35	T. Dobzhansky, *Mankind Evolving*, pp. 346–7.
19	19	"Culture is our parallel mechanism of heredity." As Tax has put it: "Culture is part of the biology of man . . . even though it is passed on socially and not through genes. It is a characteristic of our species, as characteristic as the long neck of the giraffe." S. Tax, *Evolution after Darwin*. Vol. 3. Chicago: U. of Chicago Press, 1960.
19	20	Dobzhansky, *op. cit.*, p. 22.
23	28	Huxley, *op. cit.*, pp. 11–12.
25	9	Adolf Portmann, *Animals as Social Beings*, pp. 75–6.
26	1	*Ibid.*, p. 126.

Chapter III

| 28 | 11 | Freud, *Inhibitions, Symptoms and Anxiety*, pp. 139–40. |
| 32 | 29 | "the incest barrier . . .": Freud, *Totem and Taboo*, 1913. |

Page	Line	
35	3	S. Rado, 1956.
35	35–6	"Primary narcissism" is the traditional terminology of Freudians; "magical omnipotency" is a concept popularized by Sandor Rado.
37	4	More sophisticated psychoanalytic readers may question my early memory, seeing it as a "screen memory" protecting against a more threatening awareness. And so it may be.
45	5	E. Fromm, *The Art of Loving*, p. 6.

Chapter IV

47	4	For discussion of early imprinting, see Lorenz, 1937.
47	12	For discussion of vision in the first days of life, see T. Wiesel and D. Hubel, 1963; and H. Barlow and J. Pettigrew, 1971.
51	22	For a more complete discussion of obesity, see H. Bruch, 1957.
52	25	For discussions of peptic ulcer, see F. Alexander, 1947; Thomas Szasz, 1949; and F. Kapp, M. Rosenbaum, and J. Romano, 1947.
55	21	Case of Dora: S. Freud, "Fragment of an Analysis . . .", 1905.
56	12	For discussions of nonsexual aspects of homosexual fantasy, see L. Ovesey, 1969; I. Bieber, 1962; and J. Marmor, 1965.
57	2	For the importance of the feeding situation, see M. D. S. Ainsworth, 1969; E. E. Maccoby and J. C. Masters, 1970; and R. Sears, 1972.
57	25	The relationship between nuzzling, licking, and initiation of physiological functions in the young is described in H. L. Rheingold, 1963, and A. Montagu, 1971.
58	1	Bowlby's work became an important influence on a whole generation of developmentalists, starting with his 1958 paper.
58	25	Harlow's work on monkeys (1958, 1959) had a profound potentiating effect on Bowlby's work.
59	6	Harlow stated: "The surrogate mothers (warm and soft) not only gave their infants attachment and comforts, but surprisingly enough imparted to them a very considerable degree of security and protection when the infants were placed in a strange and frightening situation." Harlow, 1963, p. 11.
59	11	Harlow, 1965; G. A. Griffin and H. F. Harlow, 1966; Mitchell *et al.*, 1966.
60	17	H. Sullivan, 1953, 1956.
60	31	For studies of the effects of institutionalization, see R. A. Spitz, 1945; W. Goldfarb, 1945.

Page	Line	
61	22	For animal studies, see L. Hersher *et al.*, 1963; P. H. Klopfer *et al.*, 1964.
62	11	Klaus *et al.*, 1970.

Chapter V

64	17	B. Jowett (ed.), *The Symposium* (New York: Tudor Publishing Co.), pp. 315–18.
68	5, 11	Bowlby, 1969, p. 223; 1973, p. 201.
68	32	Sears, 1972, p. 14.
70	9 ff.	Response to human voice: P. H. Wolff, 1963; response to human face: Spitz, 1965; speed of response: H. R. Schaffer and P. E. Emerson, 1964 A and B.
70	17	Ainsworth, 1963, demonstrated the inverse relationship between attachment and crying.
71	1	Dobzhansky, 1955, 1962, offers a particularly eloquent introduction to modern theories of human genetics.
71	18	Ainsworth, 1969, p. 999.
71	30	H. F. Harlow and M. K. Harlow, "The Affectional Systems."
72	5	For a discussion of the effect of institutionalization, see Spitz, 1965.
72	21	Peer bonding in orphans, A. Freud and S. Dann, 1951; in animals, Harlow, 1963.
73	4	This example is from M. S. Mahler, 1968.
73	28	D. Burlingham and A. Freud, 1944, p. 46.
73	32	Harlow, 1963, p. 25.
74	29	Sullivan, 1953, p. 6.
75	17	Sears, 1972, effectively makes the case for the crucial nature of early attachment.
76	22	J. Kennell, M. A. Trause, and M. Klaus, n.d., p. 12.

Chapter VI

79	3	I am here using "attachment" as formulated in J. L. Gewirtz, 1972.
81	31	On the importance of quality of relationship, see Ainsworth, 1967.
81	35	Bowlby, 1973, p. 181, states: "Children who have been well mothered, and have been protected from the experience of

Page Line

both intense distress and of intense fear, are those least susceptible to respond with fear to situations of all kinds, including separation."

82   27   On absence of anxiety as a sign of attachment failure, see Ainsworth, 1972.

83   6   For discussion of cognitive development, E. Spelke *et al.*, 1973; defensive structure, J. Robertson and J. Robertson, 1971; experience with strangers, Schaffer and Emerson, 1964.

84   1   Monkey studies influencing Bowlby: B. Seay, E. Hansen, and H. F. Harlow, 1962; Y. Spencer-Booth and R. A. Hinde, 1966.

84   21   Reassurance of familiar objects, C. Heinicke and I. Westheimer, 1966; photography, Robertson and Robertson, 1971; toys, Rheingold, 1973.

85   33   Harlow, 1963.

86   15 ff.   The research on one-year-olds reported by M. D. S. Ainsworth and B. A. Wittig, 1969; on two-year-olds, by Maccoby and Feldman, 1972.

87   26   May, 1969, p. 376.

88   11   White, 1964.

89   7   Ainsworth, 1963, p. 103.

89   23   Confidence discussed as early as T. Benedek, 1938.

89   26   The role of the mother in building confidence: "The continued existence of a reliable mother . . . makes it possible for the infant to be alone and enjoy being alone, for a limited period." Winnicott, 1958.

90   33   Spitz, 1965.

91   24   Hospitalization effects on infants: Schaffer, 1958; comparison of one- and two-year-olds: Bowlby, 1973.

Chapter VII

98   24   Freud on identification: See Freud, 1900, 1917, 1921, 1923.

100   13   Erikson, *Childhood and Society*, p. 256.

102   31   "Primary identification" as defined by Mahler, 1968. The mother as an extension of the infant in Greenacre, 1958.

102   36   Jacobson, 1964, p. 40.

103   21   Lichtenstein, 1961, 1964.

104   1   For the relationship of acting out to unconscious wishes of the parents, read A. Johnson, particularly Johnson and Szurek, 1952. Margaret Mahler, 1968, p. 19, expressed it this way: "It is the specific unconscious need of the mother that activates,

Page   Line
out of the infant's infinite potentiality, those in particular that create for each mother 'the child' who reflects her own unique and individual needs."

104   15   Mahler, 1968, p. 18.
104   20   Mirroring: Elkisch, 1957; echoing: Lichtenstein, 1964.
104   25   For discussion of the incipient sense of self, see B. Bettelheim, 1969.
106   7   The imprint of early experience on later identifications in S. Ritvo and A. J. Solnit, 1958.
107   35   Regression: Jacobson, 1954; "hatching out": Mahler, 1958, p. 68.
108   13   Freud, 1930, pp. 64–5.
108   34   J. Sandler, 1960.
109   3   Jacobson, 1964, p. 65.
109   10   J. Kagan, 1958, stated: "An individual may identify with the model not only to reduce an anxiety over anticipated aggression from a model, but also to experience or obtain the positive goal states that he perceives that model commands."
109   16   Schaffer, 1968, p. 157, expressed it thus: "Despite all the hazards of external dependence on other persons, and all the temptations to develop a splendid and objectively productive self-sufficiency, the ultimate pleasure possibilities are greater, the ultimate mastery more secure, and the ultimate growth more luxuriant when object relationships are combined with identifications." A similar feeling is expressed under the concept of empathy by C. Olden, 1953, 1958.
110   38   For a discussion of imitation, see Kagan, 1958.
111   11   The influence of identification on: attitudes—Beres, 1968; values—Meissner, 1970, 1971, 1972; self-representation—Sandler, 1960, Sandler and Rosenblatt, 1962; motivations—Schaffer, 1968.
111   19   Ritvo and Solnit, 1958.
112   1   Mutual relationships in Modell, 1968.
113   20   Mead, *Mind, Self and Society*, p. 229.

Chapter VIII

116   16   Mark Twain, *Huckleberry Finn*, pp. 331–2.
118   20   One of the few psychoanalysts who did attempt to make a systematic analysis of emotional states was Sandor Rado. See Rado, 1956.

Page	Line	
120	13	Buber, *The Knowledge of Man*, pp. 123–4.
122	34	Unconscious sense of guilt: Freud, 1907; analysis of the anal character: Freud, 1908.
125	17	Tillich, *Conscience: Theological and Psychological Perspective*, C. Ellis Nelson (ed.) Paramus, N.J.: Paulist Newman, 1973, pp. 291–2.
128	5	"Identification is known . . .": Freud, 1921, p. 105.
128	8	Freud develops his concept of conscience in: Freud, 1923, 1926, 1930. Others who have contributed significantly are: Hartman, 1960; Sandler, 1960; Hartman and Lowenstein, 1962; Jacobson, 1964.
128	29 ff.	Derivation of the superego: Freud, 1923.
130	4	For a sensitive and enlightened analysis of student rebellion from a psychoanalytic point of view, see R. Michels, 1971; R. Liebert, 1971.

Chapter IX

139	4	Reflex responses of mother in: Barnett *et al.*, 1970; Klaus *et al.*, 1970; Kennell *et al.*, n.d.
139	23	Kennell *et al.*, n.d., p. 176.
144	36	Fromm, 1965, p. 33.
145	8	The generic nature of love has long been analyzed by philosophers, and there is a rich literature on the various kinds of love, from which psychoanalysts could learn: Moffett, 1929; Nygren, 1953; D'Arcy, 1956; DeRougemont, 1956; Singer, 1966; Williams, 1968.
145	12	Williams, *The Spirit and the Form of Love*, p. 2.
146	1	Singer, I., 1966, *The Nature of Love*, p. 322.
147	33	Fromm, 1965, p. 53.
148	11	Twain, p. 317.
150	18	Montagu, 1971, p. 1.
150	36	On self-licking in rats, see Roth and Rosenblatt, 1965.
151	6	Montagu, p. 22.
151	23	Montagu, p. 110.

Chapter X

154	16	The grief-depression analogy was first drawn by K. Abraham, 1911.

Page Line
156   7   Freud's first discussion in Freud, 1917.
156   16   Predisposing personality factors in depression: Rado, 1928.
157   25   Kierkegaard: I had read this particular translation in a journal without noting the source. I find it particularly eloquent in this form and have therefore retained it. A less poetic version appears in Bretall, 1963, p. 343.
164   14   R. May, *Love and Will*, p. 286.
164   27   This quote from Mazzini was from a journal kept during World War II in which I kept no citations. I have been unable to locate the source.

Chapter XI

168   1   This quote from Thomas Mann is from the same inadequate journal as that from Mazzini in Chapter X.
168   12   This refers to Kenneth Clark's famous address to the American Psychological Association in December 1971.
169   35 ff. For an elegant discussion of the opposing view, see C. Stone, 1974, and P. Singer, 1976.
170   15   Simpson, *The Meaning of Evolution*, p. 139.
171   21   J. McDermott, ed. *The Writings of William James*. New York: Random House, 1967, pp. 618–19.
173   9   Portmann, p. 70.
174   18   Erikson, *Childhood and Society*, pp. 94–5.
176   14   On the links between biology and political science, see T. L. Thorson, 1970; Masters, 1970, 1975.
176   25   Adolf Portmann elaborates on this point as follows: "All our natural abilities are appropriate to life in a small group, where clearly defined relationships can exist between its members. . . . Thanks to civilization we are today very far removed from such a state, and this has brought us to almost insoluble difficulties. Thousands of years ago the urges and emotions we still live by, if not always helpful, would yet in a small group have been mostly harmless and non-destructive; whereas today with human relationships forming worldwide nexus and an agglomeration too big to be grasped as a group, such urges have become dangerous, threatening the preservation of the species." Portmann, *Animals as Social Beings*, p. 77.
177   28   Gewirtz, 1965.

INDEX

Adler, Alfred, 124
aesthetic bias, 40
agape, 146
aggression, 100
Ainsworth, Mary, quoted, 71, 89
alienation, 77, 132, 135, 136, 163, 164
anal stage, 100, 104, 123
anger, 163; depression and, 156
angst, 18
animals, relationships with, and emotions, 142
Animals as Social Beings (Portmann), quoted, 173
anthropocentricity, 170
anxiety, 3, 6, 38; absence of, on separation, 82; and compulsive behavior, 51; as fear, 87; phobic, 43–4; separation, 39, 78, 82, 83, 86, 90, 91, 92; signal, 90
approval-seeking, 105, 106
Aristophanes, myth of, 64–5, 97
arrogance, 5, 7
atomic bomb, 6
attachment, 58, 65–6, 138; behavior of, 67, 68, 71, 72–3, 80–1; bias for, 69; early, and independence, 85–6, 87; as foundation for later relationships, 74–5, 89; and identification, 98; ingredients of, 69–70; language of, 67; and maturation, 79; need and readiness for,

72–3; physical, 66–7; and security, 79, 80, 94–5; and survival, 77, 78; *see also* caring; love
authority: conflicts with, 130, 131, 132, 133, 134; father as figure of, 128; hunger for, 134; individual and, 99
autoerotic phase, 97; *see also* masturbation
automaticity of behavior, 112
autonomy, 84, 174; *see also* independence

back-to-nature movement, 171
Barrett, William, 7
Bhagavad Gita, 18
Bibring, Edward, 159, 160, 161
boundaries of self, loss of, 107
Bowlby, John, 58, 83; quoted, 68, 84
brain, human, 15, 26, 48
Breuer, Joseph, 121
Buber, Martin, quoted, 120
Burlingham, Dorothy, quoted, 73

Cannon, Walter, 35
caring: anxiety alleviated by, 87; Aristophanes' myth about, 64–5,

caring (*cont.*)
97; capacity for, 10, 38, 39–41,
95, 172; conscience and, 129;
for the elderly, 44; failure in,
152, 153; and the good life, 164;
and identification, 108, 131; and
independence, 95; reciprocity in,
63; reflexive, 139–40, 141, 142–3;
and social order, 136; survival
and, 12, 13, 27, 34, 115, 172,
173, 180; *see also* attachment;
love
child care centers, 177–8
childhood: length of, 24–7; and
parental attitudes, 34; stages of,
35–8; *see also* infancy
Childhood and Society (Erikson),
100
child psychiatry, 108
child-rearing in Israel, 177–8
Christianity: centrality of love in,
125, 127; conscience in, 125,
126–7; indifference in, 167; as
religion of the ideal, 126
civilization: as restraint on man,
31; and social living, 123
Civilization and Its Discontents
(Freud), 31
communication, 72–3
compulsive behavior, 51, 52, 56
conceptualization, 15, 16, 18, 20,
36–7
conflict: with authority, 130, 131,
132, 133, 134; within ego, 160;
with environment, 31
conscience, 115–36; in Christianity,
125, 126–7; and fear, 124, 127,
129; Freud's thinking on, 120–4;
and identification, 126, 128–9;
and lowered self-esteem, 156;
Mark Twain on, 116–17; social,
117, 127; *see also* guilt

contact: deprivation of, 59–60, 72;
mother-baby, 139–41; skin, 139,
140, 150–1
*Contributions to the Psychology of
Love* (Freud), 97
counter-cathexis, 122
critical period, 47
culture: and adolescent behavior,
134; alienation from, 164; and
expression of emotion, 141–2;
genetic basis of, 19, 113; role
of elderly in, 22; and sexuality
of women, 21

Darwin, Charles, 9, 32
day care centers, 177–8
death, visualization of, 18, 41
defense mechanisms, 121, 122, 124,
179
defensiveness, 109
dependency: awareness of, 27, 28;
feeding and, 55; and fellatio, 56;
in hospital situation, 54; and
identification, 12; infantile, 161–
2; and maturation, 79; meanings
of, 29; nature of, 35; prolonged,
24–7, 32, 132–3; and security,
42–4, 55; and self-image, 45;
and survival, 38, 179
depression, 119, 154–5, 166, 179;
and defense removal, 160–1; and
ego reaction, 160; and guilt and
anger, 156; and identification,
155; and infantile dependency,
161–2; and sense of failure, 157,
158, 159; survival and, 162; *see
also* despair
deprivation: and alienation, 163;
contact, 59–60, 72; early, and
higher functioning, 47; economic,

deprivation (*cont.*)
132; homosexual, 55–6; light, 47, 48; of love, 39, 42; of mother-child interaction, 76–7; and socialization, 60–1
despair, 154–65, 166, 168, 169; always over self, 157; causes of, 159; in everyday life, 162–3; and hopelessness, 158, 159, 162; national, 164; self-destruction through, 163; *see also* depression
diversification, human, 23–4
division of labor, 24
Dobzhansky, Theodosius, quoted, 17–18, 19
Dubos, René, 44

eating: compulsive, 51, 52; and security, 50, 52; *see also* feeding relationship
economic deprivation, 132
efficacy, feeling of, 88
ego-building, 112
Ego and the Id, The (Freud), 128, 131
ego ideal, 124, 127–8, 129, 131; Jesus as, 126
elderly: caring for, 44; cultural role of, 22
emotion(s): cultural restrictions on expression of, 141–2; difficulty in defining, 118, 148–9; and digestion, 52–3; expression and control of, 105; human range of, 153; and institutionalization, 60–1; misunderstanding of, 118–19; neglect of, by psychoanalysis, 97; *see also* feeling
empathy, 137, 146
environment: conceptualization of,

37; interaction with, 31, 88, 101
Erikson, Erik, 88, 89, 160; concept of identification of, 99–101; quoted, 174
eros, 146
exploitation, invitation to, 17
exterojection, 143–4

failure: depression and, 157, 158, 159; of one's own making, 8–9; sense of, 4, 6, 9; symbol of, 8
fantasies, 117; homosexual, 55, 56
father: as authority figure, 128; as model, 131; *see also* parent-child relationship
fear, 87; guilt and, 119, 124, 127, 129; and maintaining order, 135; of object loss, 90, 156; of strangers, 91
feeding relationship, 48, 49, 50, 57, 63
feeling, 137–53; of being hurt, 148, 151–2, 153; of being moved, 149, 150; of being touched, 148, 149–50, 152, 153; between mother and child, 139–41; and loving, 144; and tactile stimulus, 150–1; *see also* emotion(s)
fellatio, 55, 56
fertility, 21, 22
fetalization, 26–7, 66, 78
Fichte, Johann, 10
fight-or-flight reaction, 35
fixations, 105
Frankenstein myth, 5–6
Freud, Anna, quoted, 73
Freud, Sigmund, 112, 124, 156, 158, 161; concept of ego ideal of, 127–8; domination of psychoanalysis by, 29–34; on help-

Freud, Sigmund (*cont.*)
lessness, 28, 30; instinct theory
of, 30, 31; neurosis theory of,
30, 31; and orality, 55, 56;
quoted, 28, 108, 128, 131;
sexual theory of, 20, 30, 48–9;
studies of, on love, 96–7, 108,
109; study of morality by, 32–3;
views of, on conscience, 120–4;
views of, on identification, 98–9,
128–9, 131
Fromm, Erich: concept of love of,
44–5; quoted, 45, 144–5, 147
future: anticipation of, 16, 17, 18;
anxiety about, 3

Gardner, John, 11
gender behavior, 106
gender stereotypes, 159, 177
genetic mechanism, 19; and culture,
113
gestation period, 25–7
Gewirtz, Jacob, 177, 178
globus hystericus, 51
God: abandonment of central role
of, 14–15; finding of, in self, 4;
love of, for man, 39
grief, 154–5, 156
group identification, 135, 147–8
*Group Psychology and the Analysis
of the Ego* (Freud), 127
guilt, 3, 117–18; depression and,
156; as disappointment in self,
124, 128; in Jewish theology,
125, 127; mechanism for handling, 33; and punishment, 119–
20, 127; of the scientist, 6;
unconscious, 122; *see also* conscience

Harlow, H. F., 58, 59; quoted,
71–2, 73
hate, 167; self-, 165
Heidegger, Martin, 87
Heinicke, C., 84
helplessness, 94, 172; awareness of,
37, 158, 159; and depression,
179; Freud on, 28, 30; and loss
of self-confidence, 161; power of,
38, 40–1; prolonged, 24–7, 28,
29, 30, 34; survival and, 27,
62–3
heredity, culture a mechanism of,
19, 113
homosexuality, 55–6
hope, 166–80
hopelessness, 158, 159, 162
hospital situation, 53–4, 75–7
Huckleberry Finn (Twain), 116–17
human beings: as social animals,
32, 173; special qualities of,
15–27
human nature: hope in, 179–80;
political science and, 176; positive
aspects of, 10, 11; social character of, 113–14
hurt, feeling of, 148, 151–2, 153
Huxley, Julian, 20, 114; quoted,
15, 23–4
hysteria, 105–6, 121

idealism, German philosophical, 4
ideals, 126; destruction of, 134; *see
also* ego ideal
identification, 93, 95–6, 107, 109–
13, 117; in adults, 144, 146–8;
with authority, 134; awareness of,
97; and becoming, 137–8;
capacity for, 141; and caring,
108, 131; dependency and, 12;

identification (*cont.*)
    Erikson's concept of, 99–101;
    exterojective, 143–4; Freud's view
    of, 98–9, 128, 131; group, 135,
    147–8; and love, 97, 102, 108–9,
    128–9, 131; and maturity, 101;
    and modeling, 101, 111, 112; with
    mother, 102–4, 112, 138, 139;
    with previous generation, 8; and
    pride, 135; primary, 102–3; re-
    flexive, 138–41, 142–3; and self-
    abasement, 155; unconscious level
    of, 103–4; *see also* attachment
imprinting, 47
incest taboo, 32, 33, 34, 122
independence: attachment and,
    85–6, 87; drive toward, 79–80;
    identification and, 12; paths to,
    12, 134; period preceding, 24–7;
    as step toward caring, 95
individualism, 31, 32, 174; imita-
    tion and, 107; and society, 99,
    113, 131–2
infancy, 11, 12, 25, 27, 28, 29, 30;
    critical period in, 47; specific
    treatment in, 46–7, 48
inheritance, culture and, 19, 113
inhibition, 122
Inhibitions, Symptoms and Anxiety
    (Freud), quoted, 28
instinct theory, 30, 31, 122
institutionalization, 60–1, 72
intellectuality, 20, 80
introjection, 126, 128, 131, 155;
    see also modeling
isolation, 59–60, 147
Israel, child-rearing in, 177–8

Jacobson, Edith, 103; quoted, 109

James, William, quoted, 171–2
Jeffers, Robinson, 169
Jehovah, 125–6, 127
Jesus Christ: and centrality of love,
    125, 127; as ego ideal, 126
Jung, Carl, 124

Kennedy, Edward, 41
Kierkegaard, Soren, 157, 158
Klaus, Marshall, 62, 76, 139
Knowledge of Man, The (Buber),
    quoted, 120

lability, 70–1
labor, division of, 24
language, 15–16, 22; of attachment,
    67; and love, 145
law and order, 135, 173
learning, capacity for, 16
Leibnitz, Gottfried Wilhelm, 69
libido theory, 30, 35, 97, 121
Lichtenstein, H., 103
licking stimulation (in animals):
    perianal, 57, 150; self, before
    giving birth, 150–1
light deprivation, effects of, 47, 48
Lorenz, Konrad, 11
love: Aristophanes' myth about,
    64–5, 97; capacity for, 10, 38,
    39–41, 102; and dependency and
    survival, 38; development of,
    65–6; exemplified in Jesus, 125,
    127; founded on early attach-
    ment, 74–5; Freud's view of,
    96–7, 108, 109; Fromm's con-
    cept of, 44–5, 144–5, 147; and
    helplessness, 172; and identifica-
    tion, 97, 102, 108–9, 128–9, 131;

love (*cont.*)
indifference and, 167; and language, 145; meanings of, 144–6; and mutuality, 112; nature of, 64; need for, 28; self, and love for others, 110, 136, 173; test of, 108; vulnerability and, 111; withdrawal of, 42; *see also* attachment; caring

tion of child and, at birth, 75–7; *see also* attachment; parent-child relationship
mothering, 57, 58–9, 61–2, 69–70, 71–2; disorders of, 76; effect of separation on, 76–7; quality of, 81–2
moved, feeling of being, 149, 150
mourning, 154–5, 158
mutation, 19

magical omnipotence, 37
Mahler, Margaret, 104
man, as discontinuity, 11, 14; *see also* human beings
Mann, Thomas, 167; quoted, 168
mastery, sense of, 88, 90
masturbation, 50–1, 55
maturity: achievement of, 12; attachment and, 79; existence following, 21–2; identification and, 101; separation and, 79–80, 93
May, Rollo, 87; quoted, 164
Mazzini, Giuseppe, quoted, 164
Mead, G. H., quoted, 113
medicine, technology and, 8
mobility: physical, 22–3; social, 7–8
modeling, models, 126, 131; destruction of, 134; identification and, 101, 111, 112; *see also* ego ideal
Montagu, Ashley, 150; quoted, 151
morality, 32–3, 126
mother: autonomous rights of, 84; identification with, 102–4, 112, 138, 139; importance of presence of, 86; internalized symbol of, 91–2; psychic sense of, 91; separa-

narcissism, 98, 161
natural law, 175
Nature of Love, The (Singer), 145; quoted, 146
Nazis, 167
neurosis, 16, 121; dependency as, 35; Freud's theory of, 30, 31; symptoms of, 42
"no way out" situations, 43
nurture: and nature, 70; nature of, 45, 46–63; personhood and, 63; *see also* feeding relationship; orality

obesity, 51
object loss, fear of, 90, 156
object relationship, 98, 110
obsessive behavior, 42, 56, 155
obsessive personality, 105, 106
Old Testament, 125, 126, 127
omnipotence: delegated, 37–8; magical, 37
orality, 36, 48, 49, 51–2, 55–7, 100, 104
Ovesey, Lionel, 56

paranoia, 16–17

parent-child relationship, 34, 37–9,
57–9, 112, 138, 139, 143, 144,
145–6; reciprocity in, 61–2; *see
also* father; feeding relationship;
mother; mothering
personality: disorders of, 107;
"hereditary," 106; hysterical,
105–6; and identification, 111,
112; obsessive, 105, 106; polarities of, 104–5
personhood: dependent on relationship, 172; destruction of, 163–4;
development of, 63
phobias, 42–4
Piaget, Jean, 69, 91
placenta, 77
play activity, 88
pleasure, 48, 49, 121; of self-sacrifice, 134; sexual, and reproduction, 20
politics, 176
Portmann, Adolf, quoted, 25, 173
"post-maturity" existence, 21–2
prediction, 16, 17, 18
prejudice, 148
pride, 88, 109, 135, 136, 159,
161
primal horde theory, 32, 33
proprioceptive sense, 36, 57
pseudohomosexuality, 56
psychoanalysis, 89–90, 91, 104,
108, 112; assumptions of, 42;
attitudes of, toward love, 96–7;
Freud and, 29–34; neglect of
emotions by, 97; problems of,
130–1
psychodynamics, 130–1
psychopaths, 61, 72, 104
punishment: guilt and, 119–20,
127; to maintain law and order,
135; self-, 155, 156

Rado, Sandor, 35
Rawls, John, 166
reaction formation, 122
rebelliousness, 130, 131, 132, 133,
134
religion: abandonment of, 7; conscience and, 125–7
repression, 121, 122, 124
reproduction, liberation of sexual
pleasure from, 20
reticulate evolution, 23, 114
right-of-nature movement, 169
Ritvo, S., quoted, 111
rootlessness, 147

sacrifice: of a child, 39; self-, 134
safety: illusion of, 44; public, 135;
see also security
Sandler, Joseph, 108; quoted, 108–9
science: and culture, 18–19; and
guilt, 6; success of, 5, 6
scientific revolution, 14
Sears, Robert, quoted, 68–9
security: and attachment, 74, 79,
80, 94–5; and dependence, 42–4;
emotion and, 105; food and, 50;
in group, 148; and homo-
sexuality, 56; loss of, and depression, 162; masturbation and, 51;
oral substitutes for, 51
selective breeding, 9
self, sense of, 36, 96, 104, 112, 176;
see also identification; personhood
self-confidence, 87, 88, 92, 95, 109;
loss of, 159, 161
self-denial, 134
self-destruction, 163
self-esteem, 12, 109, 110; decline

self-esteem (*cont.*)
  in, of mankind, 3–5, 6; decline
  in, of individual, 155, 156, 158,
  161; and identification, 111
self-fulfilling prophecies, 10, 170–1
self-hatred, 165
self-image, 45, 107, 172
self-indulgence, 134
self-love, 45, 51; and love for others,
  110, 136, 173
self-pride, 88, 109, 135, 136, 159,
  161
self-punishment, 155, 156
self-respect, 124, 136
self-reward, 51, 134
sentiment and sentimentality, 142
separation, 79–93; adaptive value
  of, 106–7; attachment a step
  toward, 80; cumulative effects of,
  84, 85; from home, 44; intra-
  psychic, 87; and maturation, 79–
  80, 93; mother-child, in hospital,
  76–7; and mothering responses,
  62, 76–7; reactions to, 81–2;
  symbols of, 41; toleration of, 92
separation anxiety, 39, 78, 82, 83,
  86, 90, 91, 92
sexuality, 20–2; Freud's theory of,
  20, 30, 48–9
Shelley, Mary, 5
Shelley, Percy B., 179
Sickness Unto Death, The (Kierkegaard), quoted, 157
signal anxiety, 90
Simpson, George Gaylord, quoted,
  170
Singer, Irving, 145; quoted, 146
skin contact, 139, 140, 150–1
slums, 135
smoking, 52

social conscience, 117, 127
socialization, deprivation of, 60–1
social living, 32, 123, 173
society: identification with, 135;
  individual and, 99, 113, 131–2;
  male-oriented, 133, 159
Socrates, 64
Solnit, A. J., quoted, 111
speech, 15–16
Spitz, René, 90, 91
Studies in Hysteria (Freud), 121
sublimation, 122
sucking, pleasure of, 49
suicide, 157
Sullivan, Harry Stack, 60, 68;
  quoted, 74
superego, 131, 156
survival: attachment and, 77, 78;
  caring and, 12, 13, 27, 34, 115,
  172, 175, 180; and dependency,
  35, 38, 179; and depression, 162;
  food and, 49, 50, 63; helplessness
  and, 62–3; learning the means of,
  105, 106; and pleasure needs, 49;
  and social structure, 32; species
  and individual, 115, 123, 137
swallowing, compulsive, 51
symbolism: attachment, 74; capacity for, 15, 16, 17; of failure,
  8; of love object, 157, 158; of
  mother, 91–2; Narcissus myth,
  98
Symposium (Plato), 64
symptoms, meaning of, 162

taboos, 32, 33, 34, 122, 123
tactile stimulus, 150–1; *see also*
  licking stimulation; skin contact

Taylor, J. Lionel, quoted, 150
tears, contagious quality of, 41, 141
technology: capacity for, 18–19;
    expectations of, 5; medicine and,
    8; problems created by, 6–7, 8;
    and prolongation of dependency,
    132
tenderness, 60, 68
tension, relief of, 50–1
*Three Essays on the Theory of Sex-
    uality* (Freud), 31, 48
thumb-sucking, 49
Tillich, Paul, quoted, 125
Totem and Taboo (Freud), 32–4,
    123
touched, feeling of being, 148, 149–
    50, 152, 153
*Touching, The Human Significance
    of the Skin* (Montagu), 150
trust and mistrust, basic attitude of,
    89–90, 100

Twain, Mark, 116–17, 120, 148

ulcer patients, 52–3, 54
uniqueness, 11

variability, human, 23–4
violence, 132, 163, 169
vulnerability, 111, 159

Westheimer, I., 84
White, R. W., 88
White, T. H., quoted, 11–12
Williams, Daniel, quoted, 145
woman's movement, 176–7
women: life expectancy of, 22;
    sexual pleasure in, 21
writing, invention of, 22

A Note on the Type

The text of this book was set in Electra, a type face designed by William Addison Dwiggins for the Mergenthaler Linotype Company and first made available in 1935. Electra cannot be classified as either "modern" or "old-style." It is not based on any historical model, and hence does not echo any particular period or style of type design. It avoids the extreme contrast between thick and thin elements that marks most modern faces, and is without eccentricities that catch the eye and interfere with reading. In general, Electra is a simple, readable typeface that attempts to give a feeling of fluidity, power, and speed.

W. A. Dwiggins (1880–1956) began an association with the Mergenthaler Linotype Company in 1929 and over the next twenty-seven years designed a number of book types which include the Metro series, Electra, Caledonia, Eldorado, and Falcon.

Composed, printed and bound by American Book–Stratford Press, Inc., New York, New York. Typography based on a design by Virginia Tan. Binding design by Joy Chu.